The
TROUBLE
with
GUNDOGS

The
TROUBLE
with
GUNDOGS

PRACTICAL SOLUTIONS TO
BEHAVIOURAL AND TRAINING PROBLEMS

Margaret Allen

THE CROWOOD PRESS

First published in 2023 by
The Crowood Press Ltd
Ramsbury, Marlborough
Wiltshire SN8 2HR

enquiries@crowood.com

www.crowood.com

British Library Cataloguing-in-Publication Data
A catalogue record for this book is available from the British Library.

ISBN 978 0 7198 4279 5

Photographs by Nicky Woods: Frontispiece (Golden Retriever coming with hen pheasant) p.12 (top); p.14 (top left, top right); p.55 (bottom); p.103 (top and bottom); p.104; p.108; p.128; p.139; p.143; p.145; p.146; p.147; p.148; p.149; p.157.

Photographs by Charles Bradfield: p.81; p.120 (right); p.138; p. 142.

Acknowledgements
I have been training gundogs for more than fifty years but I feel that I have done as much of the learning as the dogs have. By watching dogs and how they act and react in different situations, I have had the best teachers anyone could have. Huge thanks to them. (And, by the way, I am still learning!)

I am very grateful to my veterinary surgeons, Matthew Bowditch and Terry Girling, and their colleagues, who have helped me to identify when certain problems are health related.

In order to offer more than one option with a problem, I have picked the brains of many friends and acquaintances to find out what they would do in certain situations. Sincere thanks to you all.

Having said that, there is one very good friend whom I must mention, and that is Douglas Jackson. It is a great sadness to me that he died before my first book, *In the Bag! Labrador Training from Puppy to Gundog* was published. He was an immense help and inspiration and did some of the proof reading. He was also full of ideas for this book on problem solving. He used to help me with my classes – even throwing dummies at age 94. He had a terrific sense of humour. When he saw a handler and dog that were completely at odds with one another, he would say, 'What a pity they have never met!' What an accurate comment – we are all different and every dog is different. We cannot hope to get on with every other human, and we have even less chance of understanding every dog. But many of us try, and usually we are not disappointed.

Great thanks to Nicky Woods and Charles Bradfield for their super photographs. Thank you as well to everyone who has allowed me to use photos and stories of their dogs' misdeeds to illustrate faults. No names, no pack drill!

To those handlers who have asked for help with gundog training difficulties, who have listened to me and used the methods I suggest, and overcome their problems, I say a very big 'Thank you!'.

Results, like actions, speak louder than words. If other trainers see that my methods work, it has to be good for gundogs as well as for their owners.

Typeset by Envisage IT

Cover design by Blue Sunflower Creative

Printed and bound in India by Thomson Press Limited

CONTENTS

FOREWORD

In a somewhat extensive life, largely spent with guns and rifles in a variety of sporting scenarios, I have owned and mostly enjoyed a number of assorted Labradors and spaniels. I have said 'mostly' because my initial attempts at gundog training were basic, and while I tried to absorb articles, books and advice from well-meaning friends, I fear that I caused more potential problems than I solved. It was not until I met Margaret Allen that I really began to understand the basic elements of gundog training and to appreciate dog psychology. This is the vital element that Margaret employs in her highly successful first book, *In the Bag! Labrador Training from Puppy to Gundog*.

Now, after a breather, she has completed her second book, *The Trouble with Gundogs: Practical Solutions to Behavioural and Training Problems*. This, in my opinion, is a book of vital importance, not only for the first-time gundog owner and trainer, but for anyone with a working gundog of any age. Here, in detail, Margaret has assembled fourteen chapters that cover in detail the numerous problems that are likely to be encountered, not only for the new gundog owner but also the many trainers who have confronted a dilemma when training their dog. She deals with every aspect of the learning process in working gundogs, including canine psychology, health and food troubles, different dogs for different jobs, equipment, commands, signals and their meanings.

Margaret covers a variety of innate troubles, such as noisiness, aggression, nervousness and fear. She tackles aspects of troubles at home and away, such as depraved appetite, unpleasant habits, playing with hazardous items and travel sickness. Problems in basic training, including heelwork, the sit and the recall, are addressed, not forgetting perhaps the worst problems of all: stock chasing, running off, and hunting for itself.

In advanced training, solutions are offered for handling troubles concerning quartering, the retrieve, the delivery, competition troubles and picking up. There is a section on hazards, injuries and illness, feeding, training for courage, and lastly, some notes about the elderly dog. Preparing and training for the dog's fitness and stamina in the field is emphasised. Never have a tired dog, writes Margaret, and always have a first aid kit to deal with potential injuries in the field.

If you are intending to train a young gundog, whether it is your first time or if you are already experienced, this book is absolutely essential. How I wish I had had a copy in my hands all those years ago!

Tony Jackson

PREFACE

My first book on gundog training was about 'getting it right'. This one is about 'putting it right'. People rarely come to me with a young, well-bred dog that is still a blank canvas, ready to go forward without any hitches. They come because they have arrived at some difficulty and are looking for a solution.

I have a good idea of what most readers will do when they first pick up this book. I have done it myself. They will go straight to the Index and look up the problem they have encountered. Then they turn to the page that deals with it. While I hope you will find that this is a book you can dip into and find help, I also sincerely hope that you will read the first four chapters at an early stage, especially the section on 'The Physiology of Learning' in Chapter 2. Understanding and implementing this will put all your dog training on a firm footing.

Some humans are natural trainers, but others need to really concentrate in order to learn to 'read' their dog, to anticipate what it will do, and to gauge when to correct and when to praise. A trainer also needs to know his dog's temperament and treat the dog accordingly. For instance, a soft-natured dog needs more sympathetic handling than a brash, boisterous animal.

Over the years, people have brought me many different dogs with many different problems, hoping that I can help. Having first established that the problem is not caused by ill health, I usually have something to suggest, something that I have used successfully with my own dogs or with dogs in training with me. You may find some of my ideas controversial, but they are offered in the knowledge that they work, and in the spirit of trying to help both dog and handler.

Although humans have altered dogs outwardly in remarkable ways by selective breeding, our domestic dogs' instincts and way of learning have changed very little since their days of living in a wild pack. Having watched dogs interacting with each other and using what I have learned from this, I have developed ways of teaching and re-teaching dogs that reflect the ways dogs themselves use. These methods are humane, and dogs understand them.

Unless I am speaking specifically about a bitch, I use 'he', 'him' and 'his' throughout the book. This is for brevity's sake and means both dog and bitch.

A mixed bag of attentive gundogs, ready for action.

Introduction

I once met a Canadian cattle rancher shooting at one of the top shoots in England. He had just flown in by helicopter from Scotland where he had been fishing and deer stalking, and the week previous to that he had been playing golf near Seattle. It was at a time when cattle farming in the UK was at a low ebb, so I remarked that things must be much better in Canada. He replied that cattle had always been a great love of his, but added, 'If you want to make money in life, choose something you like and get real good at it, but if it's cattle you like, you better get real good at something else as well!' He confessed that he had a nation-wide haulage business as well as his ranch.

How do you 'get real good at' something? Well, if you do a lot of something, you can't help but get 'real good at it'. Also, you must *want* to do it. Ask yourself what you do best and you will see immediately that whatever it is, you are good at it because you do it a lot. You strive to improve. It may be sailing, or cooking, or tennis or typing, but whatever it is, you know that you must set about it in the right way. This means that you need good information and sometimes supervision.

How do you choose good information? I think 'gut feeling' comes into it, and it is helpful if you have a natural aptitude for the subject and enjoy it. If your chosen subject is gundog training, go to classes, with or without a dog, and listen and watch carefully. You learn more by listening than by talking, and more by watching than by acting. Weigh up what appeals to you, and what you think will work for you and your dog. You need to develop the ability to sift out what you think you can't use, and to retain what you can. This requires a degree of experience – but that will come of its own accord as you proceed.

Read as much as you can on the subject, but again, you need to discern what is practical and useful, and what is nonsense. Just because it is written on paper or appears on the internet does not mean it is true. There are DVDs and online courses you can use, but again, you need to be able to sort out what you think is sensible and effective.

Most people seem capable of using a computer. This is probably because computers are made to 'think' like us – made by Man to 'think' like Man. Therefore it is no surprise that most of us can manage these complicated machines to some degree. But this book is about dogs, and dogs do not think as we do. They are not made by us, nor are they like us. We have to learn how they think. We need to get on to their wavelength.

Let's assume you have acquired a promising young prospect and you start off with high hopes. The two of you make an excellent start and steady progress. But somewhere along the line, something happens that breaks the chain. Trouble can be caused by all sorts of things. Illness of the handler or dog may interrupt training. Business commitments can affect time available. Sometimes, and it can seem extraordinary, just one careless move can confuse a dog and cause a problem. The trainer's intelligence and education may have little to do with preventing problems in training or his consequent despondency.

Lack of planning and observation are two of the chief causes of problems in dog training. However, bad timing is probably the most common cause of all.

It is clear to me that in dog training, good timing is critical. To some people it comes naturally. They are good observers. They notice the subtle changes in a dog's stance, his tail and ear carriage, his general demeanour. They watch carefully to make sure that things are going well and to see when things are about to go wrong. They act quickly, fairly and consistently. They plan a training session in advance and always end on a good note.

I have met many people who dislike using food as an aid to training their dog. They just seem to prefer to do things the hard way. In my opinion, if you find a quick way to get an idea across to a dog, that is the best way to get him to understand it. It is also the way to make the idea stick in his mind.

It is in our hands to make a success of our dog. He does not wake up one morning and say, 'I'd like to be a good dog.' We take the lead – in both senses of the term – and we set the programme. In training, we are channelling his instincts to our use, and in many cases, what we want goes against those instincts. It is up to us to convey to him what will please us. We need information, discipline and a plan. We need to learn how dogs think so that we approach them in ways they understand.

Training a dog with a problem is very time consuming and needs real perseverance on your part. You therefore have to be prepared to devote time and tenacity if you wish to succeed. If you do not have the time or determination, it may be best to find another home for the dog.

Some of the trouble we have with canines can be put down to simple incompatibility – a personality clash. Or you may acquire a dog that is just not the right material, or one that has had some traumatic experience that has so deeply affected his outlook and behaviour that it cannot be overcome. It makes him useless as a gundog. Some faults may have become so ingrained that no amount of remedial work will remove them.

You should not struggle on out of a sense of duty or stubbornness. You should not persevere out of a feeling that you are letting down either the dog or yourself. Some dogs will just not 'make the grade', however well-bred or expensive. Face the truth and find him a kind home where less is expected of him. Of course, you may be very fond of the dog and there may be family feelings to consider, but there is someone else whom that dog will suit very well, and there is another dog that will suit you ideally. Having a new dog will help everyone to get over this, and the unsuitable dog will be happier in a less pressured home.

We cannot make more time: your time is your life, so spend it on the right dog.

THIS BOOK

Although we are always learning, some things remain constant. The basics of canine psychology and of training dogs are given in my first book, *In the Bag! Labrador Training from Puppy to Gundog*. Although the title uses the word 'Labrador', the principles given in that book can be applied to any domestic dog, but they will work best with our gundogs because they have been bred to want to be gundogs. It is a book about getting things

right from the very beginning, all the way through to the production of your fully trained gundog, and I urge you to read it.

Many, if not most, problems in gundog training occur because what we want from our dog runs counter to his instincts. For example, we want him to wait patiently for our command to go and hunt or to retrieve. His instinct is to set off immediately he receives a stimulus. In our attempts to curb a dog's instincts and channel them to our use, we must see things the way he does and steadily but firmly guide him into our ways. Seeing things through the dog's eyes will be the quickest route to our goal. Observing dogs, therefore, in their interactions with each other and to their surroundings will teach us much about their ways of communication with their own kind, and their perceptions of the world in general. You will soon see that their world is one of split-second decisions, conditioned reflexes, and almost totally black and white concepts and ideas.

A dog can get his own way by going against us, using physical strength and speed, or cunning and deception. However, through careful management and training we can show him that if he complies with us, he will gain his goal. Our aim is to create a partnership. This partnership is a combination of companionship, cooperation, the sharing of skills and talents, pleasure and pride.

When trying to rectify a problem, decide on a solution and stick to it. The exception to this rule would be to discard the chosen method if it causes an additional problem. Nothing is without side effects and while some of these may be good, some of them will be undesirable.

Give your chosen remedy a fair try – not for just one training session, not for just a day or a week, but until you see an improvement. You should continue in that method indefinitely for two reasons. First, so you rid *yourself* of your old ways and become set in new ways, thus avoiding doing what perhaps caused the unwanted behaviour in the first place. Second, so the new behaviour becomes set in the dog. This will make it less likely that he will revert to his previous ways. Many people decide too quickly that a method is not working because they don't see an immediate improvement. They give up and try something else. Some things take time to work, and constantly changing your approach will just confuse your dog and make matters worse.

Nowadays, political correctness is all the rage. However, we must remember that this is a human concept and applies to human relationships. We think and understand in human ways. Dogs think and understand in very different ways to us. They live in an either/or world – if this, then that. They live in the present, thinking forwards only to their desired goals or the avoidance of unpleasantness. Their chief goals include food and freedom – these are both physical concepts. So for example, the retrieve would come under the heading of food. Hunting and sex would come under the heading of freedom. Unpleasantness also needs to be physical for a dog to respond to it. This is covered in detail in the section 'Canine Psychology' in Chapter 2.

Dogs also enjoy fun and affection, and using these we can guide them into cooperating with us.

CHAPTER 1 'Horses For Courses'

Our modern domestic dog, and our working gundog in particular, has been developed for us over many generations by our predecessors, who have chosen to breed from animals showing friendliness, attentiveness, sensitivity, gentleness and playfulness. These qualities make a dog biddable and easy to train. In addition, breeders have selected dogs that are known for their stamina, their desire to retrieve, their athleticism and their soundness – mental as well as physical – their silence, scenting ability, diligence, pace and style.

There are a number of gundog breeds, and each has its speciality. Some breeds have a higher proportion of dogs that are flighty, some have more individuals that tend to be dominant, while some are more biddable. Dogs from certain breeds tend to mature earlier than others and are better able to concentrate than those from some other breeds. Our gundogs have been bred selectively over hundreds of generations from pack member types, not pack leader types. This means that they remain trainable throughout their lives because they have a juvenile attitude and are naturally submissive.

DIFFERENT DOGS FOR DIFFERENT JOBS

Once you have decided to acquire a dog to work in the field with you, take plenty of time and care in choosing the breed, colour, sex and temperament best suited to the type of work the dog will be required to do, and which suits your temperament, personal circumstances and preferences. There are hundreds of different types of dog in the world, and every single dog has a different character and disposition.

Your choice of dog may be the cause of the problems he develops. You may have chosen a very active spaniel to be a peg dog, but he will have other ideas. Training him to be patient and steady at the peg will be hard work, and he may never truly accept this role. Or you may have chosen a German pointer for picking up in woodland on a shoot

English Springer Spaniel, known in days of yore as 'the maid of all work'; he is best when in full employment because if left with time on his hands he can be very mischievous.

with several adjoining drives. But it may be extremely difficult to keep a far-ranging dog in a tight radius, and the fear of him encroaching on the next drive is ever present.

The spaniels should hunt close to their handler. They flush and retrieve game and are small, so they can wriggle

11

An English Springer Spaniel in action. His job is to hunt, flush and retrieve.

A lemon-and-white working Cocker Spaniel. Cockers come in many colours and it can be difficult to predict what a certain mating will produce. These dogs were originally used for flushing woodcock, hence the shortened name; they are deemed to be experts on this particular quarry.

into thick cover, and can fit with several others in the back of a shooting brake.

The retriever breeds vary in size, colour and coat texture. They are worked on all types of terrain – moorland, woodland, estuaries and ponds, hedges, ditches and in game crops. They may be required for driven shooting or duck flighting, walked-up game or rough shooting.

White-and-black working Cocker Spaniel. This breed can be very lively, mentally and physically. They need to be firmly taught the boundaries from the outset or they can make life very trying for the owner.

Four different retrievers: Chesapeake Bay, Flatcoated, two Labradors, with a blue-roan Cocker in between. This last is my favourite colour of Cocker.

A black Labrador dog, strongly built, which looks as though he could do a hard day's work.

These two Golden Retrievers are sister and brother and I had them both as pups. They are beautiful and polite, and terrific game finders.

A yellow Labrador bitch. She is neat, balanced, and strong but feminine.

The British pointers and setters have been developed for questing over wide areas where stamina and scenting ability are paramount. They must come on point when they scent game, and be steady to flush and shot. These breeds are not usually expected to retrieve, although I have seen several that were more than willing to do so.

Labrador puppies at four and a half weeks. Note the difference in the set and shape of the ears of these puppies compared to the Viszla pups in the next picture. The pigment of the nose and around the eyes is also much darker.

Hungarian Viszla puppies at seven weeks. These pups will grow up to be taller and finer coated than the Labrador or Golden Retriever.

A Golden Retriever pup of eight weeks. Note the coat is thicker and longer than the Viszlas' and the Labradors'. Golden Retriever puppies often carry their tails high at this age but it usually lowers.

A Flatcoat in action. Flatcoats usually love water; the problem may be in persuading them to come out!

A Flatcoated Retriever dog. This breed can be challenging to train as they have their own ideas. Their scenting and marking abilities are usually outstanding. They are fast, good at jumping, and strong swimmers. They make loyal companions.

An Irish Water Spaniel with friends. She has her fringe tied up with a bow to allow her to see more clearly. This breed is, in fact, classified by the Kennel Club as a retriever.

An English Setter. This is one of three types of British setter. The others are the Gordon, which is usually black and tan, and the Irish, which is a bright coppery red. There is also the Irish Red and White Setter, but this is rarely seen nowadays.

The Weimeraner, originating in Hungary. This is one of the hunt, point, retrieve (HPR) breeds, sometimes called the Grey Ghost. They are one of the more popular HPRs in Britain.

A German Shorthaired Pointer, in the less usual colour of solid black. The more common colouring seen in the UK is liver and white in patches and spots. The breed also comes in a wire-haired variety.

A Munsterlander dog – another of the HPR breeds. The male is often bigger than the female. Both need imaginative training as they can become bored very easily.

The hunt, point, retrieve (HPR) breeds have been developed in countries other than Britain. They vary greatly in size, the Brittany Spaniel probably being the smallest and the Italian Spinone one of the largest. There are different coat textures to choose from – smooth, rough and long haired. The range of colours is vast, and traditionally, most HPRs have their tails docked by about one-third to two-thirds.

There are other gundog breeds, such as the Nova Scotia Duck Tolling Retriever, which does a rather specialist job. This dog trots about in the shallows where ducks gather, and his waving tail seems to intrigue the ducks. They follow the dog, which lures them towards the Gun so they are within shooting range before they are put to flight. Afterwards, the dog retrieves the downed game. This group includes the Dutch Kooikerhondje, which works in a similar way, its jauntily held tail enticing ducks into a complex cage system where they are trapped.

As a general rule, minor breeds – that is, breeds that are not numerically strong – are minor for a reason. This is usually because they are not as biddable or easy to train as other breeds. Another reason can be that the breed suffers with certain hereditary health problems, or a lack of longevity. You should do your research thoroughly in all these aspects before making your final choice.

As if it were not enough to have such a wide choice of breeds, there are variations within each breed. There are the show types and the working types. Show representatives tend to be larger and more heavily built than their working

An Italian Spinone. Like all the HPRs, and the setters and pointers, these dogs are bred to range at great distances from their handlers. This makes these breeds less than ideal for use in lowland driven shooting.

Three eager faces not wanting to miss a thing!

cousins. Their trainability has sometimes been neglected in favour of looks. The Labrador breed has many examples of the two different types. English and Irish Setters, English Springer Spaniels, Cocker Spaniels and Golden Retrievers all have quite a rift between the two types. Having said all that, they are still all dogs with canine instincts and the desire to be part of a pack. Some are easier to train than others. The working types tend to have had their talents preserved and honed, whereas the show types have had their working potential ignored to a degree.

Remember that every dog is an individual, and selecting the dog with the temperament to suit you can add to the complexities of making a choice.

You may well be able to see now why pedigrees are important. If you want a dog for work, try to find one from good working bloodlines. This may require quite a lot of research and enquiry. If you need a particular type and temperament, you should seek the advice of someone who has been involved with your chosen breed for a long time and who knows the different families. Some people will have their own agenda when advising you, so don't be in a rush. Weigh up all the information you can glean before making your final decision. Careful choice of your dog at the outset may help you to avoid many of the problems addressed in this book.

CHAPTER 2 The Learning Process in Dogs

It is very helpful to understand how we learn, and how dogs learn. For this reason I begin with the physiology of learning. Please read this more than once so that you gain a really strong hold on it. It is very important.

THE PHYSIOLOGY OF LEARNING

Learning is the establishment of long-term memory. The physiology of learning is how we *physically* learn. Researchers have discovered certain proteins in the brain that make long-term memory possible. These proteins and others are associated with learning, and they exist in the brain not only of dogs, but of humans and other animals too. When a physical activity is performed, electrical activity is created in the brain. This electrical activity stimulates the special proteins, and they in turn assist in the laying down of connections or what we might call 'pathways' between the brain cells. These pathways are the basis of long-term memory. The pathways are made more concrete and lasting by two things: Repetition of the activity, and Rest afterwards.

Any memory is made more lasting by these two things. They may be good memories or bad ones. So if, for example, a dog spots a deer and chases it across a couple of fields and into a wood, it will tire him so that when he gives up on the deer, he will need a rest. If this sequence is allowed to take place again, you have the two elements that help to make a strong, lasting memory: Repetition and Rest. In the case where the dog is successful in catching and killing the deer, we can also add the element of Pleasure. Repetition, Rest plus Pleasure without Unpleasant Physical Consequences equals a really worthwhile event in a dog's mind. Therefore in training, we must do our utmost to *ensure that what a dog learns is what we want him to learn*. We must not permit the repetition of activities we do not want a dog to remember. We must prevent undesirable pathways being laid down in his brain. We must not allow him to indulge in activities we

do not want to become habits. Habits are hard to break. Some habits are impossible to break.

If your dog succeeds in doing something you do not like, be sure that as soon as possible, you do some concentrated, positive training in a confined area for about six minutes. Give him time to calm down first, of course, and make sure you have control of your temper. You must deal with the dog fairly and in a way that will make him enjoy the training. You can be lavish with treats. Be sure to finish on a good note, and then put him away in a quiet place for at least an hour. Let a 'good' activity be the one he remembers.

Dogs cannot learn in abstract ways as we do. They do not attend lectures, listen to the radio, read or watch television. Dogs learn through *physical* association. That association may be pleasant or unpleasant. It could be fun, soothing or delicious on the one hand; on the other it could be frightening, painful or embarrassing. Because of this, we must use methods that a dog easily understands. The best ways are those that he learned from his mother in his early life, and this is covered in the next section.

It is also true that an extreme event in an animal's life can result in the very quick or even immediate grasp of a concept. If an experience is very pleasurable, such as chasing a deer, or very frightening or painful, such as being shocked by an electric fence, it will not need many or any repetitions for the long-term memory of the event to be formed. A sharp lesson will work better than all the nagging in the world. Similarly, an especially enjoyable experience will stick in his mind. So make sure his pleasant experiences fit in with your plans, and that his disobedience meets with meaningful correction.

CANINE PSYCHOLOGY

Some people treat dogs like children. Some treat them as equals. Others treat them with roughness and brutality. Some spell dog backwards.

The association between man and dog is very old and based on how each can be of benefit to the other. Dogs find ways of gaining a place in our lives. They work out what we like and dislike in order to gain what they want from us. They show us affection and amuse us, warn us and guard us, bring things to us. We like the feel of them and the look of them. Their superior senses, athleticism and stamina provide a wonderful extension to our abilities.

Training could be defined as the methods by which we harness their talents so that they are of use to us.

What we humans learn in our early days is what we learn most thoroughly, remember most clearly. We are born with human instincts. We tend to be brought up by, and taught by humans. We learn how to learn in human ways. That sticks with us.

It is much the same for dogs. They are born with canine instincts, and their first learning is usually from their mother, who is a dog. They learn how to learn in canine ways. That sticks with them.

When we wish to communicate with dogs, we do not have a common language. It is not even like trying to communicate with a human foreigner who does not speak our language. We have to find other ways to get our ideas across. We must try to understand the canine ways of teaching and learning. We need methods and we need 'tools'.

Observing dogs' interactions with each other can teach us much about how they may react to and interact with us. Watch a bitch with her puppies and you will see how she disciplines or encourages them. Watch how two dogs, strangers to each other, establish who is to be the superior dog in their relationship. This varies according to age, sex and whether either dog is a natural leader. Watch young dogs at play, or a bitch in season with other bitches, and then with a dog. You will see many signs and signals – some are easily understood, others are very subtle. Time spent watching dogs is time well spent if we are to succeed in building a good working relationship with them, if we want to discover the 'tools' that will work best in a training programme.

Making it seem a reward when we give a dog his food, spending time stroking, grooming and fussing him, all the while talking to him in a friendly, praising sort of voice – these things give a dog the physical association with our kind voice. Thus we have a 'tool', our pleasant voice, and we can use this 'tool' to convey to the dog when we are pleased with him in a training situation. If he complies with a command and we say 'Good dog' he thinks, 'When I hear that tone, it usually feels or tastes nice. I must remember what I have to do to reach the "Good dog" part.'

Equally, we need a tool, a *physical* association, to tell the dog when we are not pleased and to deter him from actions we do not want. He needs to learn what our cross voice means, *physically*.

In the wild pack system, the nicest physical association a dog might encounter would be to be licked clean and dry by his mother as a puppy, to have a wound or infection licked by a peer, or perhaps to enjoy some mutual grooming. The best they can expect as a reward for good behaviour as an adult would be to be ignored, something to be grateful for but not much of a 'tool' to help in training, looking at it from a human point of view.

The physical corrections or punishments to which a dog would respond best are those that he would have learnt in his early days from his mother or other adult. More correctly, these should be called 'demonstrations of dominance'. Like us, what dogs learn when they are young is what sticks with them, so it is important that what your dog learns in the early stages is what you want him to remember.

The earliest lessons a dog learns are about dominance and submission so that he fits into the hierarchy of the pack. As most of us know, dogs in the wild live in a pack system. There is presently a popular belief that the pack structure is a myth, but there is too much anecdotal evidence showing that it exists. In my opinion it cannot be denied or ignored.

Over the thousands of generations of dogs, the pack leaders have developed several stylised behaviours that are designed to embarrass and sometimes hurt, but not harm, 'naughty' pack members, to 'put them in their place'. They do not wish to harm them because they need their help and cooperation. It is not just the leaders that use these behaviours – adults of lesser standing will use them on youngsters and puppies.

The stylised behaviours, or punishments as we might call them, consist of displays and acts of dominance. The displays of dominance include the superior dog holding himself stiffly erect, especially his head. His tail will go up and may vibrate slightly. He will walk with a stiff-legged gait. He will look directly at the offending pack member or members, and he may growl threateningly. The acts of dominance are usually extremely swiftly administered – usually a short, sharp bite and shake of the insubordinate dog's scruff. With persistent offenders, this may be repeated several times with increasing severity, and blood may be drawn – but seldom is any real damage done, either physical or psychological. Over the generations, dogs have come not only to know when and how to administer these punishments, but also, if they are the recipients, to understand and therefore not to fear them. They will also know how to respond to them in order to show their submission and end the punishment.

We are speaking here of dogs that are members of the same pack, dogs that know each other. With intruders, there may be nothing stylised about it, and blood may flow! But even in such situations, if the intruder acts in a submissive way, he will probably be tolerated, if not accepted.

THE MUZZLE-HOLDING TECHNIQUE

Young puppies are taught by their mother at a very early age to respect their elders. She teaches them the meaning of the muzzle-holding technique. This technique was designed by dogs, and while it is a very mild form of punishment, interestingly it is one of the most effective demonstrations of dominance that a dog will use on another dog.

A mother dog, when annoyed by a lively puppy, will cover his muzzle and perhaps his eyes with her mouth and press down, growling fiercely. She may also place a forepaw on his neck or shoulder to hold him still. She does not bite the pup, she just holds him still. The pup reacts by lying very quietly on his side or back, wagging his tail apologetically. He may also show his submission by urinating, something he may do for very little reason, even for us! After a while his mother will release him, slowly, but still growling. Usually the youngster will leap up again straightaway, just as annoyingly as before, and the whole performance will be repeated. If the puppy persists, the mother dog may eventually give him a sharp nip, which leaves him yelping and sorry for himself, but not traumatised. Other older dogs may treat a youngster in this way, and eventually the pup learns that a growl is a warning of worse to come if he continues to annoy.

This demonstration of dominance can be used by us as a 'tool' that is effective in the training and management of a dog for the whole of his life. From a hygiene point of view, we would not wish to have a dog's muzzle in our mouth! However, we can use our hands instead to gain the same effect. One hand should hold the dog by the collar or scruff at the back of the neck, and the other should be placed over the dog's face. The thumb should be on one

side of the muzzle and the fingers on the other. The pressure on the muzzle is firm but gentle – it is *never* a grip or a pinch. The technique is most effective if the dog's eyes

The handler holds the collar to steady the dog while covering the muzzle with her free hand. Please note that although the collar should be held firmly, the hand on the muzzle must only be placed lightly. Covering the eyes can make the muzzle-hold even more effective, as it makes the dog feel disadvantaged and puts the handler 'in the driver's seat'.

The handler should exert gentle downward pressure on the dog's muzzle, and should keep the dog still for up to ten seconds before slowly removing the hand from the dog's face. This technique gives the dog confidence in his handler, calms him, and causes him to concentrate. If the dog resists you, persist until he accepts. Do not resort to force or roughness at any point; just be calmly determined while holding on to the collar firmly.

are partially or entirely covered. You must not hurt the dog, only hold him still. You should speak sternly but not loudly to him.

If your dog shows signs of submission, you should continue to hold him for about seven seconds more, and then slowly let him go. Signs of submission would include becoming very still, showing the whites of the eyes, panting and/or smiling, licking the lips, putting the ears back, lowering the tail and half-hearted tail wags. Yawning is also a sign of compliance. You will often see this after you have released your hold.

Dogs with a fairly brash nature may resist the muzzle-holding technique. If a dog tries to dodge the hold, take a stronger grip on the collar or scruff, pressing downwards, while the other hand remains gently over the dog's eyes. The pressure on the eyes and muzzle should always be light and almost soothing. Speak quietly but firmly. Your aim is to gain the dog's acceptance of you as his superior, so you must resist any temptation to be rough. You want him to be your team mate, so do not frighten him. Take your time and do not let him go quickly. When you do release him, do so very slowly.

As you take your hands off his neck and muzzle, put the lead on; keep your face averted, and be silent for up to a minute. Then start to speak nicely to him, stroking him above eye level but with your face turned away from his. Touching him above eye level shows you are 'top dog'; below eye level would be seen by him as you being submissive. Looking him directly in the face would be perceived as confrontational; looking away is the aloofness of the leader. You will find that he is happy to be friends with you. The use of this technique teaches him the physical meaning of your cross voice.

Thus you have the 'tool' you need when you have to convey to him that you are displeased. He will want to avoid being in your bad books if at all possible, so he will tend to correct himself when you speak crossly. He will be inclined to strive for 'Good dog' status.

The muzzle-holding technique is a very useful tool that shows a dog that you are in charge; it calms an anxious dog and makes a flighty dog concentrate.

THE 'OFF SWITCH'

At the end of each training session, put the lead on your dog and take him to his quiet place. Your lead is the 'off switch'. When on the lead, your dog does not have to be responsible for his actions – except that he must not pull on *your* lead – so he can relax and the laying down of firm memory pathways can commence. You should also put the lead on your dog during training sessions whenever he has performed an exercise well. Doing this for three or four minutes will result in his feeling at ease and gives the memory pathways a chance to begin forming.

In more advanced training, when your dog is steady, taking the lead off 'switches him on'. He will learn that the lead being removed means that he must pay attention and focus on what is happening around him. For instance, take the lead off when you want him to mark a thrown dummy.

If you set your dog free at the end of a training session – and I know how tempting it is to reward a dog for good behaviour by letting him have a scamper – he will fill his eyes, ears and nose with information and his mind with

This is a happy dog, confident in his handler and anticipating fun.

ideas that run counter to your lesson, and he will forget what you were trying to teach him. Free exercise should *precede* a training session. At the end, put the lead on him and make him know you are pleased with him – that is his reward

THE QUIET PLACE

After every training session, remember that your dog needs to rest. He may not be physically tired but he needs a spell on his own. The training will 'sink in' while he is resting. Memory pathways will be formed and strengthened. You can have a few 'quiet places' where he can be shut in after each training session. This might be a cage in your utility room or in your car, or it could be a kennel that you can close, and which limits his view.

He should not have toys, chews, food or a companion. You want him to think about his lesson and not

be stimulated by his surroundings. Put him in his quiet place for ten to sixty minutes, out of sight of any activity, to 'think things over'. This sounds anthropomorphic, but it does work (see 'The Physiology of Learning' section at the start of this chapter). The next time you have him out, his last lesson will usually have gelled and you can build on this and make forward progress.

When a client comes to me for a training session I explain the physiology of learning, and as he or she is leaving, I say, 'Don't have the radio on during your drive home. You need quiet time for the lesson to gel in your mind too.'

PRAISE AND PUNISHMENT

My approach to dog training and rehabilitation is based on observation of dog behaviour. I believe that this has led me to a fairly clear understanding of canine psychology. The methods I use are not always 'politically correct'

A good-sized cage for a spaniel or retriever that will suit the average puppy almost to adulthood. It has a plastic tray on the bottom and you should place bedding of some kind on it. Always ensure there is drinking water present.

but I believe they imitate the ways of the wild pack where higher echelon dogs mete out swift physical punishment for the misdemeanours of lower-ranking pack members – but at the same time, they are usually consistent and fair. Their punishments are tailored to the crime and the age of, and their relationship to, the miscreant dog. Dogs do not, however, praise each other or give a good dog a pat on the back. The best a lower level pack member can expect is to be ignored. Humans can think beyond this. We can give credit where it is due: we can give praise, pats and treats when a task is performed well. This tends to boost the speed of the learning process. Humans can also use equipment such as the collar and lead, whistles, dummies and 'the quiet place' to assist in the education of their dog.

It is important to remember that the things a dog does that we consider 'wrong' are nearly always due to him wanting to follow his instincts or to gain our attention. If we are to be successful in channelling his instincts, training him, we will have to show him that to comply with us is beneficial and preferable to him than to follow his natural inclinations.

In order to communicate with your dog, speaking to him, kindly or crossly, is not enough because dogs need to have a *physical* association with our voice in order to understand the meaning. This way of learning is hard-wired into the mind of every dog. Your different tones of voice must have physical associations.

Many people think that applying physical correction or punishment will damage the relationship they have with their dog. On the contrary, dogs respect the one who shows leadership, and in a dog's world this is the one who corrects him, physically, and guides him to reward.

Some people think it demeans both dog and trainer to punish a dog physically. That is anthropomorphic thinking. *Unless we see things the way the dog does, we will not be able to get our ideas across to him.*

Sadly, political correctness does not now allow a human teacher to touch a human pupil, even to praise or to comfort. We would not make much progress with a dog if we never touched him! He loves it when we ruffle his coat and fondle his ears. Suppose someone gave you a bag of gold coins; surely you would not say just 'Thank you!' You would be thrilled: you would shake his hand and let him know how delighted you were! Be like that with your dog – show him you are pleased. Make your praise sound sincere. Abandon reserve and let your hair down!

Many readers will have seen programmes on television where dogs with severe behavioural problems are 'cured' using 'positive reinforcement', usually in the form of food and treats. Other positive methods involve using alternative options such as distracting the dog from what interests him. This is fine in its place, but with our gundog we need to create an attitude in the dog of self-discipline and cooperation whereby he knows that if he obeys his handler, he will achieve his goal. His goal is usually the finding of game or a retrieve. Self-discipline means he acts against his instincts when under temptation so that he is under his handler's control at all times. Cooperation means he acts in concert with his handler for an enjoyable shooting outing.

Treats do have a place in training, but a dog has to be food-oriented, perhaps even hungry, for bribery to work. When a dog is excited, food has little or no appeal. If offered a treat during a drive at a shoot, many dogs will not even look at it. Alternative rewards may work in certain situations but you need to know how to weigh up the level of appeal. For example, offering a dog the distraction of a trip in the car as opposed to chasing a deer, the deer wins every time.

There are occasions where I advocate giving a dog a light slap. Some people say that hitting a dog is foreign to him and not something he can learn from or understand. This is simply not so. In his daily life a dog may be struck in many ways. You might throw a few biscuits in the grass for your dog and some may hit him; he will think the touch well worth accepting! A door or gate can accidentally close on him; an object can roll off a table and land on him. When following his handler or another dog or when chasing an animal through undergrowth, he may be struck by a branch which has been pushed forward and let fly back. Even a flick in the eye by another dog's tail can be painful. There are many instances when a dog is hit in life and he either accepts it or learns to avoid a repetition by being more attentive, watchful and cautious.

If a dog is given a sharp tap on the side of the muzzle in conjunction with cross words, he will associate the hurt and surprise with the scolding. You may never have to repeat the physical treatment with a sensitive dog – one short sharp lesson will stick with him. A dog needs to have a physical association with his trainer's tone of voice; a pleasant one connected with praise and endearments, and an unpleasant one connected with a warning or scolding.

Another form of correction that I use is the check chain. It is a pity that this training aid is often called a 'choke chain' or 'choker' because this gives the wrong impression. The chain collar should never be used to choke a dog. The handler should use it to give a quick correction and allow the chain to loosen immediately. The check chain is preferable to other collars or slip leads because the noise it makes when it is tightening warns a dog of what is to come and once he understands this, he will correct himself when he hears the sound of the first few links as the handler takes up the slack in the lead. The noise makes the check chain a fairer and kinder form of correction than the silent rope or leather slip lead. *See* the section in Chapter 4, 'Equipment'.

Any dog with a problem should wear a snug-fitting buckle-on type of flat collar so that the handler can take hold of him easily without hurting him. The handler can easily hurt a dog when grabbing him by the scruff, and this can quickly make him hand shy. Once hand shy, a dog can become very difficult to catch. If you take hold of the collar, you can scold and correct, and when you see contrition, you can make up with the dog. If you cannot catch the dog in the first place, everything is delayed and the misdemeanour may be long forgotten by the time you do arrest him.

You must use just the right amount of physical correction. Too gentle and the dog will not respond – at first he will view it as nagging and quite soon it will be as unimportant to him as wallpaper. Too much and you may dull his senses, or you could create fear and mistrust. Err on the side of caution to begin with, but if you do not gain the response you want, you will need to be tougher. Immediately he gives the desired response, you can return to praise and reward.

There are many successful trainers who use harsh methods to achieve results. We all have our own views about such methods and the people who use them. My opinion is that harsh methods are not needed if the *initial* training is taken steadily, step by step, so that the dog understands what is required, and also what is not, through every section of his training. However, this is a book on solving training problems and it is very easy to install a problem unintentionally. If it is a serious, life-threatening problem – such as running off – which has become an entrenched habit, the solution may require the handler to employ very firm methods to overcome it.

Timing is vital with both correction and reward. Both need to be given at the exact moment the trainer sees the dog is about to act or react. Dogs live in the here and now. It is useless to punish a dog after the event – he cannot make the connection between his misdemeanour and the punishment. This is why I am reluctant to mention the use of the electric collar. A shock given a moment too soon or too late can be disastrous. Praising or rewarding a dog at the wrong moment will do little or no harm, but praising him before, or even a short while after he has performed well, will not mean anything to the dog. He will certainly like it and it may aid the bonding process, but it will not teach him that the deed he performed was the one you wanted.

Generally speaking, I have found that the firmer you are with dogs, *physically,* the more they seem to love you. Tough, boisterous dogs become focused and compliant. Soft dogs seem to gain confidence from firm handling and their trust and affection for the trainer increases. In both cases, this is because dogs are pack member types and firm handling tells the dog that he has found his leader.

By 'firm' I do not mean rough, but you should always insist that the dog does what you say. For example, if you give the command to sit and the dog refuses, say 'No' and physically and firmly put him in position. Say 'Sit' again and praise him, stroking him at the same time. You have come to the praise part quickly. This speeds up the learning process, and what is learnt quickly is learnt well.

BE THE PERSON YOUR DOG CAN TRUST

It is vital that you always try to see things the way the dog sees them. You need to show your displeasure at the exact moment he transgresses, and respond with praise the instant he looks compliant. He needs to be able to understand you and trust you. He needs to learn that you will be friendly the instant he obeys, so do not go on grumbling after he shows cooperation. It can be difficult to change from cross to friendly instantly, but it is possible and you can train yourself to do it. You must become something of a Jekyll and Hyde character, and change to the right person according to your dog's actions and reactions.

MAKE WHAT YOU WANT PREFERABLE

The first rule to understand in dog psychology is that dogs only do what they find preferable. We humans would like to follow this rule too, but we make ourselves do the distasteful things because we know that

Time spent bonding with your dog is time well spent. Go down to his level and make a fuss of him, just because you can.

doing them will make our future better. For instance, we wash the dishes so we have clean ones to eat off later. We will get up early to catch the train to work because being late has so many negative consequences. Dogs are more immediate, but they do have a concept of 'if this, then that'.

We can teach dogs to do things that go against their instincts by making what we want preferable. Training is balancing praise and correction – rewarding actions that please us, correcting the converse. If you add the muzzle-holding technique to your sessions, the dog will become calmer and concentrate better. He will be more accepting than he otherwise would be.

BE THE LEADER

Canine pack leaders use body language and facial expressions to show their superiority, and we can imitate many of these in order to impress the dog we hope to train. In a domestic situation, a dog feels happy and confident when he knows his correct position in the human 'pack', and this is best learnt early in life. The pack leader always maintains a position that is physically higher than the pack members. Pack leaders do not approach from below the eye level of a pack member. A canine pack leader that is offended by a pack member will look directly into his face and growl, he will stand tall and stiff, possibly with his lips curled and teeth showing. The irritated mother dog of a boisterous pup will stand as tall as she can, keeping her muzzle raised and an aloof expression on her face. If the annoyance continues, she will charge the whippersnapper and pin him down with the muzzle-holding manoeuvre.

Keep all this in mind when you look directly at a dog; does he perceive it as a threat? An example might be when you return to him after the 'Sit'. He may have stayed absolutely still, but if you stare at him he thinks you are displeased and moves in self-defence or rolls on to his back. After all, that is how you returned to him on a previous occasion when he had moved out of the 'Sit' – you stared at him, you were not pleased with him, and you put him back crossly where he should be. If this is the way things went, he will almost certainly be worried if you return to him 'full face'. Now you know why. Return to the dog with your chin up, face slightly averted – he will probably remain in place.

Wrong. When you are teaching a dog to remain still while you go away, you should not look directly at him on your return. This handler is staring at the dog full face, which will almost certainly make the dog think he has done wrong and he will then move. If he does, you will have to correct him and start over again.

Right. If your dog has remained where you left him, return to him, chin up and looking over his head. He will find this reassuring and remain still. You will have done the exercise correctly.

DOGS ARE QUICK

It is important to keep in mind just how quick dogs are – quick thinking and quick acting. It behoves us to be as quick as we can to gain their respect and cooperation. For example, if you watch your dog closely you will perceive when he is about to 'go wrong', and with quick responses you may be able to prevent trouble and therefore be in a position to praise instead of scold.

In the same vein, a dog's responses can be immediate when it suits him, and so they should be immediate when it suits us. For example, if a dog sees a squirrel running on the ground, he doesn't look at his watch to check the time. He's off! His response is immediate. If we ask a dog to sit, his response to our command could and should be immediate.

UNDERSTAND YOUR DOG SO HE CAN UNDERSTAND YOU

If you are new to dogs, you must take time to study them and learn to 'read' them. It will pay dividends if you make time just to watch. Dogs will show you what they intend to do next in a number of ways. Their facial expressions may be limited, but they show a great deal with their ears, eyes and tails, the shape of the body and their gait.

You need to react in the appropriate way to the signals your dog gives. Go to training classes and watch other

handlers with their dogs. Ask for advice. A happy, confident and compliant dog almost smiles at you; he wags his tail and his ears seem to say, 'What do you want me to do next?' A wary dog will show the whites of his eyes, his head and tail are held low, and he slinks or runs away. The lowered head and tail also show when a dog is ready to cooperate with you. You need to be able to tell the difference. Dogs live in the moment, and if you remain in scold mode when he has shown contrition, he will not know when he is right. It may make him think that he is never right. It can make him fear you, and you may lose his trust. Learn to read his expressions and his body language. What he is thinking and how he feels shows in very subtle ways, but in time you will learn to interpret the signs.

Dogs can be very intelligent, some more than others. They have the capacity to learn many skills, which allow them to enjoy life and improve their lot. Our gundog breeds have been developed over many generations to want to do gundog work: it is not work to them, it is what fulfils them and makes them happy. However, much of the time their enthusiasm to do the work makes them impetuous, and if not channelled and controlled this can

The first training class of the year. Some dogs have their focus on their handler, some are less attentive.

spoil everything on a shoot day. It is our job to teach him that managing his enthusiasm is in his own interests.

Because dogs do not see things the way we do, and we cannot explain it to them in words, it is up to us to see things from their point of view if we are to gain their cooperation and compliance. We have to show them that there is benefit to them in being a team mate. We have to understand them and how they perceive the world. Of course you can gain compliance through force and intimidation, but the best working relationships are based on mutual respect and affection between partners.

If you think about your training sessions before you start, you can make a step-by-step plan for that lesson's exercises. With a plan, you have a good chance of success. The dog will not have a plan; he is just happy to be out with you – and why not? It should be fun to go out together. Even though you are channelling his instincts and bending him to your wishes, it should result in an enjoyable experience.

If you reach an impasse and your dog persistently disobeys you, you must ask yourself why. Does he really understand what it is that you want and why you are displeased? Sad but true, the answer is that it is your fault. If you are at a loss to understand what is wrong, it may be that you should give your dog what an old friend of mine called 'wholesome neglect'. After ending your training session with a very simple thing you know he will do, even just the 'Sit', put him away and do no further training for several days or even a week. Put your mind to the problem, seek advice from someone you respect, and do not tackle the difficulty until you have figured it out. Meanwhile, your dealings with the dog should be friendly and pleasant, just

These dogs have found a good vantage point.

attending to the essentials of life. Keep him in enclosed spaces. Be gentle with him, use a soft voice, stroke and groom him and allow him to play. This will build a bond between you, and when you begin to recommence training, this should stand you in good stead.

Sometimes you will see what appears to be defiance in a dog's face and demeanour. *It is not defiance – it is lack of understanding and a readiness to run away at the sight of your apparent displeasure.* You must change tactics. Soothe the dog, put the lead on and return to the beginning; try another approach to the exercise in question. If this does not work, or if either of you has become upset over the situation, ask him to do something simple that he knows well, then call it a day. You must always end on a good note so that your dog is left with a good memory. Before your next session, think about what went wrong in the previous one, and make a plan that will help things move forwards.

DON'T BE ANTHROPOMORPHIC

Beware of attributing human ways of thinking to your dog. For instance, do not fall into that old trap of thinking that dogs know that they have done wrong. Dog owners so often say, 'He knew he was wrong. You could tell by his expression'. He did *not* know he was wrong. He just knew from *your* expression and stance that he was going to get 'what for'. He could see you were cross, but I assure you, he did not know what for! Dogs live in the moment.

Another thing I hear people say is, 'He knows he's not supposed to do it because he only does it when I can't see him!' This is a dog that has learnt that it is not wrong to do wrong: it's wrong to do it when you are present. What *you* think of as wrong is to him just something you don't like to see him do. This little wrinkle is tackled under stealing, eating dung and noise-making.

CHAPTER 3 What Is the Cause of the Trouble?

When a problem arises, we need to know why. We need to discover the cause of the trouble.

IS IT HEALTH TROUBLE?

If a dog that is usually lively and enthusiastic is listless or uncooperative, you must assume that something is wrong. When he first comes out of the house, car or kennel, he may well be excited, and this can mask an underlying state of ill health. However, when you begin training, you may notice that he cannot remember the previous lesson, or he seems lacklustre or stubborn.

It could be something very simple – perhaps you have not given him a chance to 'spend his pennies', or it may be that he has been sick in the night – dogs often eat up their vomit straightaway so you wouldn't necessarily see any evidence. Or perhaps he has a gastric upset in the lower gut – you should see diarrhoea nearby or soon after letting him out for exercise. Perhaps without you knowing it he may have been fed a large meal recently, which is making him feel bloated and lethargic. Check him over. Look carefully at his paws and move his limbs about within the normal range. If he draws his foot away quickly or gives other signs of pain, look more closely. You may find a cut or a thorn or a broken nail. A strain may not make him lame, but a day of rest may improve his vitality. He may have some kind of infection; whatever it is, you need to find out before you continue his training.

I once took a very keen dog out of the kennel for training, and after we had practised the basics, we moved on to the retrieve. I began with a simple 'seen': the dog was sent and went with a will, but when she lowered her head to pick up the dummy, she seemed to change her mind and was very reluctant to take it in her mouth. I encouraged her but to no avail. Finally, I decided to look inside her mouth. Thank goodness I did, for along the inner side of her molars a flat piece of metal with the ends turned over had caught in her teeth. She was always a great one for picking up odd things, but this was the most unusual. She was not in pain, it was not life-threatening, but it was enough to make her not want to retrieve. It is always worth looking for clues when a keen dog behaves out of character.

If a dog's nose is dry and his eye rims are dark red or, on the other hand, greyish, I recommend that you take his temperature. Normal is 37.5 to 38.8°C (around 101.2°F). If his temperature is much above or below this, I would consult your veterinary surgeon as soon as possible.

If a dog is normally cooperative and eager but suddenly is not, and there is nothing obvious to be seen, put him away in a quiet place and see how he is in an hour. If he seems no worse, I would leave training for that day and see how he is the next day. If he has deteriorated, you must consider taking him to your vet.

Skin pests can distract a dog from his training. Treat your dog regularly with veterinary-approved products to eliminate external and internal parasites.

The morning stretch. This dog is having a good stretch after waking, which means he is ready for action.

Dogs need regular worming – they can pick up worm eggs the day after the last worming! I have found that if a dog is carrying a heavy burden of worms, it can affect his behaviour. External parasites result in a dog being distracted by the skin irritation, so it is obvious that you should take steps to eradicate the pests so that the dog can concentrate on his training.

As a rule, only healthy animals stretch. When your dog comes out of his bed or kennel and has a good stretch and a shake, it usually means he is feeling well and is ready for whatever you have planned. It is worth noting, however, that a dog may stretch if he has some sort of colic.

Whatever the cause of a dog's poor performance, we need to act accordingly. We need to find out what is wrong and put it right. Then we need to wait until the dog is well enough to proceed with the training programme. In some cases, such as when a dog has had worms and been treated, a couple of days later should be fine to start training again. With a mild illness, you may be able to

recommence in a few days. In the case of a serious illness or injury, you will of course need to follow your veterinary surgeon's advice.

If a bitch has just been in season or is about to come in, you may find that she is unable to concentrate well. You always have an excuse with a bitch!

IS IT THE FOOD?

At different ages and stages a dog's nutritional requirements may and often do change. Some dogs manage best on foods with a low protein content. Others need a higher level of nourishment. Certain high-protein foods can be inadvisable for some dogs – it can be like feeding rocket fuel instead of a quality, more balanced food.

Experiment with different foods to find what suits your dog best. You should give each new food several weeks' trial to ascertain what effect it has. It will take some time for the new food to produce a change in behaviour or energy levels. Introduce each new food gradually, reducing the old and increasing the new over the course of a week or more. If a food disagrees with a dog's digestive system, you must naturally revert to a food that he can cope with.

Your dog should be reasonably hungry when you take him training – he definitely should not have had a recent meal.

IS IT A MATTER OF MOOD?

There may be nothing physically wrong with your dog. There are any number of things that could affect his outlook and mood. You should give the matter careful thought before you decide that he is just being naughty. He may just be too young and playful to grasp what you are trying to teach him. He may be over-excited because he has not had any exercise to let off steam. He may have been frightened by something you don't know about. Perhaps you are wearing clothing he has not seen or smelled before. He may be a very sensitive creature who views anything new with apprehension. He may be anxious because the previous training session ended badly and he knew you were not happy. It is up to you to work out what is wrong, to cheer him up or soothe him, and to set an achievable plan for the day's outing.

NATURE OR NURTURE?

Some problems are due to the dog's nature: they are innate. Some problematic behaviours are learned. Each problem will have its own symptoms and must be tackled accordingly.

Some problems come in tandem with one another, such as unchecked excitement leading to noisiness, nervousness being connected to aggression, compulsive food snatching leading to a hard mouth. This can mean that in treating one difficulty you may cure another at the same time.

Every dog is an individual. Each one will fall into some broad category, but each dog will have some difference in character, some quirk or quality that sets him apart from other dogs. If we are to achieve success with a dog and make him into a useful gundog, we need to find out what makes him tick, get on to his wavelength, understand him and bring out his talents.

A well-bred dog should have the talent in him to do the job for which his breed was developed. However, there are some individuals that, in spite of a stunning pedigree and excellent forebears, have inherent faults that will make your job very difficult. You must assess your dog and decide if the faults he exhibits are ones you can live with, surmount or eradicate. It may be that your temperament and that of your dog are not compatible – you may never bond with him, or you may feel it is not worth the effort to try. Time is precious, and if you feel you cannot overcome or accept his faults, it is kinder to you both to find him another home.

However, you must take the greatest care in choosing his successor. Avoid the same bloodlines – look for fresh names in the pedigree. Find someone knowledgeable but impartial whom you feel you can trust, and while keeping to your own personal preferences regarding breed, sex, age and colour, be guided by this person. There are many likely dogs to choose from, but it may take some time, effort and expense to find the right one for you.

We are impatient as a species, but this is an important choice. A hasty decision could well result in another uphill struggle with another unsuitable animal, and this will greatly damage your confidence. You should not make any snap decisions, even if a dog seems ideal. Ask the vendor if he will give you first refusal, and do not feel pressured if he says 'Someone else is coming to see him tomorrow'. Sleep on it. If it goes to someone else, there will be another dog somewhere for you. A dog should last around twelve to fourteen years, so take your time in choosing him.

IS IT YOUR FAULT?

If you are inconsistent, unclear or confusing, a dog will soon learn when he can disobey you. Perhaps

Allowing your dog to jump up or put his front paws on you leads to trouble. He may do it when he is muddy, or he may knock you over if he takes you by surprise.

The Shoot Meet, when dogs are relatively clean. The liver-and-white Springer Spaniel with his paws on his owner's coat may not be making it dirty now, but if it happens later in the day – tut, tut! The small golden Cocker Spaniel lunging on his lead could wrench her handler's arm and hurt his own windpipe.

occasionally you allow your dog on the furniture indoors – but not always. Sometimes you allow or even invite him to jump up and put his front paws on you – but at other times you scold him for jumping up. Perhaps you are amused when he leads you around holding you by the sleeve of your old jacket – but when wearing your best coat, it is not so funny. On occasion you insist that the dog should sit, and then on another, perhaps because the ground is wet or there are a lot of thistles, you do not insist that he sits. Maybe the dog sets off on a retrieve a split second before the command to go, and you allow him to 'get away with it' and soon he

is running in for a pastime! The dog is never sure when something is permitted or when it is not, so he assumes it is allowed until he is told otherwise.

Inconsistency in one situation will lead him to question you in *all* situations. You must be honest with yourself, and if any of this is true, *you* are the one who has to alter.

In summary: If a dog does not behave well, we must first rule out a health matter. After that, we must consider his age, his temperament, his state of mind, or how the previous lessons went. Ask yourself if the problem has arisen due to your lack of planning or clarity, or to poor timing or inconsistency.

It may be amusing when a dog tries to retrieve you by towing you along by your clothing, but there may come a time when he tears your sleeve or accidentally gives you a tooth butt on the wrist – not funny!

CHAPTER 4 What You Will Need

As with any job, pastime or sport, dog training requires special equipment and specific commands, whistle signals and hand signals.

A dog is an intelligent being and very perceptive. He is acutely aware of subtle changes in his surroundings and in the other living things in his vicinity. We need to realise how we appear and how we sound, and to be careful not to change things just because our mood changes. Blowing the whistle more loudly or for longer is a typical example. This is not helpful – it is just different, and a dog will not respond to 'different'. Making your hand signals more emphatic than usual is not helpful – that, too, is just different. Keep your commands in a neutral tone and try not to use them in a scolding voice. Keep your more serious or cross voice for scold words such as 'No!' and 'Leave!' – and remember, it is the *physical connection* a dog has with your tone, good or bad, that matters, not the decibels.

Make sure none of your voice commands sound like your dog's name. 'Heel' sounds like Teal but has its own meaning. 'In' and Bryn are too similar. Using names such as Bruno, Juno and Beano will devalue the scold word 'No.'

Hand signals must be clear and distinct from each other because what a dog sees is so important to him. Your hand signals must be given in the same way every time. Your body language must not be confusing.

Throughout your training regime, especially in the early stages, keep speaking in a friendly way to your dog to maintain a thread of communication between the two of you. Be sincere in your praise. Touch him from time to time, particularly on his face. Your ultimate aim is to have a willing working and sporting companion, one who enjoys being with you and who extends your abilities with his superior speed, agility and scenting powers. It is worthwhile spending time just sitting beside your dog, chatting to him and ruffling his coat.

The bond you will be forming will be a good basis for all your training.

EQUIPMENT YOU WILL NEED

Equipment includes collar and lead, whistle, dummies and a training bag, of course, but in addition you will need suitable clothing and footwear. It is no good being too cold or too hot, having uncomfortable shoes or clothes that are too tight – you do not want any distraction because you need to be able to concentrate on your dog. You will need pockets to keep treats in, to put your lead in, to carry gloves and other bits and pieces. You may need a hat to keep you warm or to shade you from the sun. A hat to shade your eyes is better than sunglasses: if your dog can see your eyes, it is easier for him to read your expressions. Be sure you are not distracted by hunger or thirst. We cannot arrange the weather, but for training, try to choose a day when you can both enjoy the outing.

Collars and Leads

When problem solving at close quarters, I advocate using a flat buckle-on type of collar and a soft lead of 1.5 to 2 metres in length. The collar should be done up so that it is snug and the dog cannot easily pull out of it. Both collar and lead should be comfortable for you to hold, and should not tighten on the dog's neck.

For day-to-day training, I prefer to use a check chain and a leather or fabric lead. Used correctly, the chain tells the dog when he is wrong by the noise it makes. The lead should be soft and broad so it is comfortable in your hand, and should be at least one-and-a-half metres long. The clip should be easy to operate – the trigger sort is

When your dog is ready to begin more serious training, heelwork for example, a check chain and soft lead have definite advantages over the flat collar or slip lead. The chain makes a noise when it begins to tighten, warning the dog to cooperate or he will feel the chain tighten. It should be used with a short, sharp tug. It should *never* be used to choke a dog. It approximates to the nip a senior dog might give an insubordinate youngster in the pack situation. This chain has been put on correctly for the handler who keeps his dog on his left. Gravity will loosen the chain when tension in the lead is released.

A flat collar and soft lead are essential in early dog training. A slip lead can frighten a young pup. There are many times a day when you need to take hold of a youngster to restrain him, and a collar is kinder and surer than taking hold of him by the scruff.

best. The check collar should be long enough that when it is put on, it rests at the base of the dog's neck just in front of the shoulder. The ring that the chain runs through should come from under the dog's neck, whichever side you lead him.

The two rings of the chain should remain together as much of the time as possible. If you can see the two rings lying together, you know the collar is loose and comfortable. If you can see 3 or 4 inches of chain away from the dog's neck, you know the collar has tightened – it should only be tightened on purpose. There should be a nice 'smile' in the lead with no hint of tension. A horseman speaks of 'a feel on the rein': this means that you can feel contact with your animal but there is no drag or pressure on him.

When a dog is learning to walk correctly to heel, the lead should hang in a 'smile'. In this way you know your dog is comfortable, and because of this, the dog knows he is in the right position. This handler should have the lead across her body in her right hand so that the left hand is free to encourage or pat the dog; also her left hand will appear as it will when the dog is not wearing a lead – the picture is so important to a dog.

Whistles

It is a good idea to have several whistles, all the same pitch and all on lanyards. One lives in the car, one hangs on a hook inside the back door, and the one you usually wear can be on your dressing table. If you have whistles of a standard make, they are easily replaced if you lose one. Your whistle should hang 3 or 4 inches above your waist so that when you lean forwards to touch the dog or take a retrieve, it does not dangle near his mouth.

Dummies

Have a selection of dummies. They should be of different weights and textures so that the dog becomes used to carrying a variety of things. It is helpful if dummies are of different colours or shapes so you know one from another. This makes it easy for you to use a separate one for each retrieve, and helps prevent the dog from becoming bored. If you have dummies that are alike, number them clearly with permanent marker so that you can tell them apart. This will also help you to come home with the same number of dummies that you took out with you! With time and use, each one will acquire its own individual scent, depending on where it has landed and who has handled or retrieved it; then, although the dummies look alike, they will seem different to the dog.

Dummies should be carried in a training bag or vest so that your hands can be free. Take care not to have too big a bag unless carrying heavy weights does not concern you. Place the dummies in the bag vertically so that it is easy to see and extract the one you want.

This handler's whistle lanyard is too long; it allows the whistle to dangle in the dog's face and mouth, resulting in them both sharing spit! Your whistle should hang about a handspan above your waist.

A good game bag. This one has a wide shoulder strap, which distributes the weight well. The main part can accommodate a selection of dummies. There are two zip pockets big enough to carry spare leads, sunglasses, or perhaps a snack. There is a net pocket for birds (two partridge or one pheasant) and two smaller pockets for a treat container and a pot of launcher blanks. It is not so big that you have room to carry everyone's dummies: that would be silly!

A pouch in the back of a training vest should be roomy and easy to access. The vest should be machine washable and quick drying.

Obviously warm weather! A good training vest has lots of pockets, a two-way zip, and is broad over the shoulders to spread the weight.

Balls

A black ball with a white mark painted on it is a good aid in teaching steadiness. When rolled along, the white mark looks like a rabbit's scut (tail) and makes the ball resemble a running rabbit. Use with the dog on the lead until he understands that he must sit when he sees the ball rolling.

Tennis balls are useful in training – they are fun and tempting, but your dog must not view them as toys. They are especially good when you are teaching a dog to hold his ground – they usually give off a good scent but can easily be hidden from sight so the dog must use his nose. A tennis-ball thrower is a light and easy gadget to carry and use.

A tennis-ball thrower and tennis balls are very useful in training retrievers. A ball seems to be very exciting to most dogs, and the thrower allows you to send the ball quite a long way. Being small, the ball teaches a dog to hunt diligently and hold an area.

This ball is solid and weighs about half a kilo. A white spot painted on it resembles the scut of a running rabbit when you roll it on uneven ground – very attractive to dogs! It is good for steadiness training.

Dummy Launcher

A dummy launcher is beneficial in the more advanced stages of training. It uses a .22 blank to propel a dummy, and there are various grades available. The more powerful blanks are very loud and give a significant 'kick' on firing. These send the dummy a long way, and are best used with a remote-controlled launcher. The least strong blanks are much more user friendly and although they do not send the dummy as far, they are adequately exciting to a dog. Take great care when introducing the launcher as some dogs are very unhappy about the sharp

The dummy launcher has limited use, in my opinion, except that it excites dogs a great deal and this can be useful when teaching steadiness. Some dogs are more fearful of the noise the launcher makes than they are of a shotgun. This is thought to be because the former makes a sharp crack and the latter makes a duller sound. According to the power of the .22 blanks used to fire it, the dummies can be propelled at greater or lesser distances, which can save time and effort on the handler's part. There are also launchers that can be operated remotely and can send the dummies in different directions. Some are propelled by pressurised air and are not noisy.

A suitable travel crate for Labradors and the smaller breeds. The dog can stand up, lie down and turn around. He has only a limited view of the world outside and this seems to reduce car sickness. This one is easy to lift and to clean.

crack of the .22 blank – *see* the section 'Gunshyness' in Chapter 5, 'Innate Troubles'. Once a dog understands it, he will usually be very excited by a launcher.

Crate or Kennel

A crate or kennel is a very useful thing to have. It prevents a dog from being destructive, and helps with house training. It can be his quiet place after lessons. It should be viewed by you and him as his safe refuge, not a place of punishment. It should be roomy enough for your adult dog to stand up, lie down and turn round in it.

COMMANDS AND SIGNALS YOU WILL NEED

Commands and Signals for All Dogs

'Sit' or 'Hup'

Meaning: 'Assume the sit position. Sit until I tell you to do something else.' This command also comes to mean 'Stop and look at me.' The dog learns to stop at a distance so that he can be given additional signals and information.

Whistle signal: One short toot for retrievers. Trainers of spaniels and the pointing breeds usually use a longer toot, about one second.

Hand signal: Hand raised to one side of your face, no higher than your forehead, with all your fingers pointing up, and your palm facing the dog. This signal shows up well at almost any distance.

Wrong. The signalling hand is too high and is too much like the signal for sending the dog further away, which is used with the command 'Get on'.

Right. The hand should be no higher than the handler's forehead. The handler's shape is very distinct.

Note: You should not use the word 'Sit' with quartering dogs if you use the command 'Seek'. The words sound too alike.

'Come'
Meaning: 'Come towards or right up to me.'
Whistle signal: For retrievers, use pairs of pips on the whistle, repeated as necessary. For spaniels and the pointing breeds, a series of pips is usual.
Hand signal: Extend a welcoming arm, or crouch to encourage the dog to come to you.

'Heel'
Meaning: 'Keep your shoulder near my knee, whether we are standing, walking or running.' It also means that the dog should face in the same direction as the handler.
Whistle signal: None.
Hand signal: Pat the front of your thigh.

When encouraging a dog to keep in the correct heel position, pat the front of your thigh. If you pat the side of your leg, it is inclined to make the dog hang back to keep out of the way.

A handler leaning slightly forwards and extending welcoming arms will be more attractive to a dog than if he stands straight and still. Things growing smaller do attract dogs; perhaps this is based on their instinct to chase prey that is running away and therefore diminishing in size.

'Run On'

This is the release command.

Meaning: 'You may suit yourself, *within reason*.' It does not mean 'Leave the county'. It means 'You may break the last command I gave you, or not, as you please.' For example, if you had told your dog to sit and then did not require him to remain sitting, and did not intend to ask him to do anything specific, you would say 'Run on' and the dog could have a scamper; or he could remain sitting if he preferred. Your dog will learn this command more quickly than any other!

Whistle signal: None.

Hand signal: A small flick of the hand.

Your chosen word or phrase should only be used to release your dog and nothing else. Alternatives might include 'Freedom', 'Playtime' or, as one of my friends says, 'Bam-a-lam'. Do not use 'OK' – it can be dangerous. We frequently say 'OK' and 'all right' without thinking. It might be said at the worst possible moment: the dog could run off into traffic or some other danger.

'Leave!'

This command is used when a dog is taking an interest in something forbidden such as poultry, cats, livestock, carrion or manure.

Meaning: 'Have nothing to do with that!'

Whistle signal: None.

Body language: Use a threatening posture.

Commands Associated with Retrieving

'Hie Lost'

Meaning: 'Go out in the direction indicated, find the retrieve, pick it up and bring it to me.' Use when casting a dog out for an unseen or 'blind' retrieve. It also means 'Pick up the article you have dropped or are anxious about picking.'

Whistle signal: None.

Hand signal: A clear hand signal close to and alongside the dog's muzzle in the desired direction.

'Get On' or 'Away'

Meaning: 'Go straight away from me.' Use when the dog is away from you and needs to go further away.

Whistle signal: None.

Hand signal: One arm raised high, giving an upward flick of the hand as the arm reaches full height.

Some handlers use the command 'Back' for this. To me, this word is too much like 'Bad' and could be confusing to a dog. Also, it is difficult to say clearly with a whistle in your mouth – you will sound like a poor

The signal for sending a dog out on a blind should be the flat hand alongside the muzzle pointing in the appropriate direction. Note that the whistle lanyard is the correct length.

The signal for 'Get on' begins with the arm raised high, the hand points downwards, and as the command is given, flicks up to its highest extent.

The completion of the signal for 'Get on'. The command is given as the hand flicks upwards, showing the dog, even at a great distance, a clear action and shape.

ventriloquist and it will come out as 'Gack'. There are, however, certain situations where I use the word 'Back', one being when we are walking a very narrow path and I wish the dog to drop back and walk behind me. Another is when, heaven forefend, a dog has jumped from the back of the car into the front – an offence I most emphatically resent! Then the word 'Back' can most definitely be understood to mean 'Bad!'

'Right'/ 'Left'

Meaning: 'Go right/left (stage right/left) parallel to my arm.'

Whistle signal: None.

Hand signal: A clear sideways signal at shoulder height with the appropriate arm. You should point a line parallel to the line that the dog must travel to reach the retrieve.

The signal for the dog to go to the right – your right, his left. The arm is raised from your side to shoulder height, and as you give the command, you lean your body to the right and waggle your hand. It often helps in the early stages to emphasise by stepping to your right as well. Remember, for both right and left, you should be pointing a line parallel to the line the dog must travel.

The signal for the dog to go to the left – your left, his right. Remember to lean sideways and waggle your hand as you say the command. If more emphasis is needed, you can take a step to your left.

Note: You should *not* say 'Go right' or 'Go left' – the dog will hear the word 'Go' and go the way he chooses, in spite of a very clear hand signal.

'Get In'

Meaning: Used for entering water: it tells the dog he should go in and keep going until he is redirected.
Whistle signal: None.
Hand signal: None, or the same as for 'Get on'.

Note: A different command should be chosen to tell the dog to go into the car or kennel, for example 'In you get'.

'Cover'

Meaning: Used to tell the dog to get into cover – woodland, bracken, thickets and so on. Many people use 'Get in' for this, but if a dog is in a situation where there is a choice, he will usually prefer to go into water rather than cover.
Whistle signal: None.
Hand signal: Directional signal if needed.

'Over'

Meaning: 'Negotiate that obstacle.' Used when jumping or climbing is required, for example fences, walls, steep banks, hedges and ditches. It also tells a dog to get out of water on the far side.
Whistle signal: None.
Hand signal: None, or the same as for directions.

With regard to work in water and cover, some trainers say that using 'Get in' as well as 'Over' is unnecessary and can be covered by using 'Get on' alone. I would not argue, except to say that I believe that dogs find the different commands 'Cover', 'Get in' and 'Over' very encouraging when they are tackling specific barriers.

'Steady'

Meaning: 'You are coming into a position where you will find the scent of the retrieve.' This command is particularly valuable when scenting conditions are difficult. You must be sure of the exact position of the article, and only say the command when the dog is downwind of it and in a position to find it. It should not be used when the dog is upwind of the retrieve: he needs to believe you are telling him the truth.
Whistle signal: Soft, repeated toots to sound like the two syllables 'Stea-dy'.
Hand signal: None, or a hand lowered to encourage the dog to hunt.

'Careful'

I use the word 'Careful' when I do not know the precise location of the retrieve but know that the dog is in the general area. I want him to feel encouraged to give the vicinity a thorough search. It is said quietly and there is no signal. I have heard a pointer handler on the Scottish moors give this command. It had an interesting effect on the Guns walking nearby!

'Dead'

Meaning: 'Bring the retrieve to my hand.' This command is traditional – often the retrieve is wounded, not dead, but these retrieves are the most important to get to hand.
Whistle signal: None.

Take delivery overhand. It is our way when receiving a gift to stretch out our hand with palm uppermost. A retrieve is a sort of gift, but seeing your open palm will cause a dog to drop what he is bringing more than anything else.

As you move to receive the retrieve, extend one hand to pat the dog on the head and take delivery with the other hand. Better still, extend the hand you intend to take the retrieve with, palm downwards, pat the dog's head, then run the same hand down the side of his face and take the article overhand.

Hand signal: Extend the hand palm downwards as if to pat him. Run your hand over his head, hold him if necessary, and take the retrieve overhand. Or when your dog approaches with the retrieve, extend your hand as if to pat him on the head – and indeed, you should pat him and then take the article with your free hand.

It is instinctive for us to extend our hand palm upwards to receive a gift or prize, which a retrieve is, but seeing your open palm will cause a dog to drop what he is bringing more than anything else.

'Brrrrrr!' and 'Mark!'

This sound and the word are not technically commands but are used by many trainers to alert a dog to the fact that a dummy is about to be thrown. The 'Brrrrrr!' sound is supposed to simulate a pheasant taking wing. A dog should be taught to sit the instant he hears this sound.

Commands Used with Quartering Dogs

'Seek' or 'Where is He?'

Meaning: 'Hunt in the given direction' when you cast the dog from beside you. It also means 'Turn' or 'Change direction' when the dog is away from you.

Whistle signal: One or two short pips.

Hand signal: Indicate the direction you require with your lowered hand.

Note: Do not use the word 'Seek' if you use the command 'Sit'. The words sound too alike, and one means stop and the other means go.

'Road In'

Used to encourage a dog on point to move forwards to flush the set game.

Hand signal: None, or your fingers clicked in front of his face.

When casting out a spaniel, or any questing dog, to hunt for unshot game, keep your signalling hand low and act in a conspiratorial manner. This handler's body language is exaggerated to show the young dog that the two of them are hunting together. You are trying to engender a sense of team spirit between you – the dog should not think he is out just to please himself. The low hand signal and body posture also differentiates hunting from retrieving in the dog's mind.

CHAPTER 5 Innate Troubles

Some troubles in a dog are due to heredity – that is to say, the dog is born with a leaning towards a fault. It is innate. Many innate faults can be alleviated or even eliminated if the trainer goes about it in the right way. However, some temperament faults are insurmountable, and the trainer must decide when to call it a day. However, if you like a challenge and eventually achieve success, you may be justly proud. It must be remembered, though, that this success does not mean that the leaning has disappeared from the dog's make-up, so when considering breeding, it is important to decide if it is wise to breed from a dog showing certain temperament faults. You should also bear in mind that an innate problem may resurface at any time in spite of all your efforts to eradicate it.

NOISE-MAKING

There are two types of noise-making. One is voluntary – the dog is consciously asking for something he is not allowed. If he is corrected consistently, he will give it up. The other is involuntary – the dog is quite unconscious of making the noise, he just does it. He has little or no control over his noise-making. If he is punished, he will still make the noise and then cringe as if to say, 'Oh, drat! There's that noise. There's trouble when I hear it!' It does not take long to determine whether your dog is making a noise voluntarily or involuntarily. If it is involuntary, he should be discarded as a candidate for gundog training, especially as this fault has a tendency to grow worse, not better.

This fault is possibly the earliest fault to show in a dog. All puppies make noise, but in a litter of puppies you may notice that, at a very young age, one is more vocal than the rest. I would mark this puppy so that you can follow its progress and see if the trait lessens or becomes more pronounced. This may be the pup you took a fancy to because of its colour, markings, size or character. Whatever the reason, let your head rule your heart.

Perhaps a puppy is not particularly noisy when with his siblings, but becomes so when he arrives at his new home. If you know he does not need to go out to relieve himself, has toys and is not hungry, you will need to address the situation.

A youngster in training may whine with excitement or jealousy when he sees other dogs working. You may be able to distract him by moving him around on the lead and scolding him quietly. Do not give him food – this would be rewarding him for making noise. Apply the muzzle-hold to calm him and make him focus on you.

The first few times you take your young dog out in the shooting field, he may whine. Indeed, he may make quite a lot of noise. Often this is because he is not quite ready or mature enough to be out in 'battle conditions'. Take him well away from the shooting, preferably out of sight. A squirt of water from a water pistol in his face may surprise him into silence and remind him that he should be paying attention to you. If he still persists, you must take him home. He is not learning anything good. Go back to an earlier training phase and take him to group sessions as often as you can. Insist that he focuses on you.

A dog will sometimes make a noise out of anxiety or fear when he first attends a shoot. This also shows that he has not had enough preparation for the field. Putting cotton wool in his ears may help to calm him, but if not, you should take him home. Return to a much earlier stage in his training and gradually build up his confidence in less testing conditions. *See* 'Unnecessary Barking or Howling' in Chapter 6.

NERVOUSNESS AND FEAR

Nervousness and fear can appear early in a pup's life. Start to socialise your puppy as early as you can and as much as you can. Take him on short walks in different places. Let him come with you in the car as often as possible. He will learn to be calm in new situations if nothing bad happens to him, so be very careful that he is not frightened or hurt when he is in a new situation. Do not have him around strange, boisterous dogs or unsupervised children. You must protect him from 'hard knocks', even accidental ones. Try to arrange things so that he is merely jostled in company at first. He needs to learn that being bumped into by other creatures is normal and although sometimes frightening, it is just part of life.

He needs to become accustomed to slight pain but not real harm. When you are grooming him, for instance, you will sometimes pull his hair a bit. If you stop as soon as you feel tension and then tease out the matt or tangle, he will become used to small amounts of discomfort and accept this as normal and bearable.

A dog cannot learn in a fearful state. He can think of only one thing, and that is how to escape from the situation. He has to overcome his fear before he can turn his mind to anything else, especially anything useful to us.

A truly nervous or anxious dog will seldom accept food. If you offer food to a dog that appears to be nervous and he accepts it, I think you may assume that he is 'trying it on': he is pretending to be frightened so you will be soft with him.

The best cure for nervousness is to demonstrate to your dog that you are in charge so that he can relinquish responsibility for his safety to you. Use the muzzle-hold and be stern. Speak in a firm but not loud voice. He must understand that he has no business to be afraid as you are in charge.

It is particularly important with a nervous dog that you plan your training sessions. An anxious dog needs a structured training plan. This does not mean doing the same things in the same order in every session – you must not have him acting by rote and you must not bore him to tears, but he needs to learn that 'this' leads to 'that' and that he can depend on your consistency. You must be consistent even though you train in different places and with other dogs and people around.

A very nervous dog or puppy should wear a flat, buckle-on sort of collar at all times as there will be many times when you will need to catch and restrain him. Grabbing him by the scruff of the neck would only confirm his fears. Attaching a short cord to the collar will help you catch him if he runs away. You should also keep him in a safe enclosure until you feel confident he will come to you, even when he is frightened.

Charlie and the Muzzle-Hold

A year-old English Springer Spaniel came to me for training a few years ago. At the age of about nine months he had been 'rescued' by a friend of mine from a pet home where he had been left indoors for eight to ten hours a day while the owner was at work. When that owner returned home, Charlie was turned out into the garden. The garden was surrounded by a high wooden fence that prevented him from seeing the outside world. He had almost no way of learning what was dangerous or what was safe. He was seldom taken for a walk because he pulled so hard on the lead and was terrified of nearly everything. He was not housetrained and would not come when called. He had had so little social contact that he did not react with friendliness to anyone. My friend brought him to me in despair. The dog was prostrate with fear, creeping along the ground, and although he was on a lead, he darted constantly towards hiding places, trying to go under cars, behind doors and into bushes.

I took him by the collar and placed my free hand over his eyes and muzzle, and after a few seconds I could feel the tension melt out of him. His owner felt it too. It was like magic. It took many weeks to bring Charlie to any semblance of normality, and some of his quirks never went away, but he became happy and confident in his owner. She did not wish him to be a gundog, which was just as well – his lack of early learning experience would have seriously hampered training for sustained obedience in the field. But the fact that the muzzle-hold could make such a difference is a testament to its effectiveness.

Before you can begin training him, you must win his trust. Be patient but determined, calm and quiet. Do not make sudden moves. Show him that he can rely on you. Use treats and the muzzle-hold freely.

A dog of this nature may benefit greatly from being neutered. Neutering may well make him calmer and easier to manage. If within six to eight months after neutering he has not become more trainable – and we are speaking here about training him to be a gundog – you should rehome him.

Sadly, you will sometimes encounter a dog that cannot overcome his nervousness. This sort is a danger to himself and to others, and he will not become a reliable gundog. It is best to find him a new home. In an extreme instance, the kindest option is to put the dog to sleep.

AGGRESSION

Most of our gundog breeds have happy, friendly, outgoing natures, but from time to time we meet individuals that can be unfriendly to the point of biting other dogs and sometimes people. In a shooting situation this is unacceptable.

Aggressiveness in dogs has one main cause – heredity. I believe aggressiveness has to be in a dog to come out. We are speaking here of the dog that, on a shoot day, puts everyone – people and dogs – on edge. This dog often attacks without any warning. He just pitches into his victim and often causes real injury. Sometimes he will guard the vehicle he is in, especially if there is game in it. Some only bite other dogs. Some bite dogs and humans. Some will guard food or things they think belong to them or their owner. Barking or growling a warning may be acceptable but attacking is not.

I always advise against breeding from dogs that are incurably aggressive. A bite occurs in an instant and a person may be scarred for life, mentally as well as physically. I speak from experience – my granddaughter was bitten in the face at the age of four years by a stray dog when she was at a beach on holiday. She needed twenty-seven stitches. The scars hardly show now and she likes dogs and is an accomplished trainer, but it is a disgrace that it ever happened.

Sometimes aggression results from a dog having too strong a guarding instinct – *see* the section 'Overdeveloped Guarding Instinct' later in this chapter. It is all right

Aggression – a Multi-Faceted Liability

A man went up to Scotland for a week's shooting and took his very unreliably tempered black Labrador bitch with him. By the third day, the dog had bitten the host's dog, the keeper's dog, and enough other dogs to make everyone in the party anxious and watchful. The owner realised his dog was worrying everyone and spoiling their fun, so when one of the Guns had to head south early, he asked him to take the unfriendly creature back with him. The Gun lived not far from the owner so it was arranged that he would take the dog home.

On the way down the motorway the driver stopped for fuel and a drink and a pork pie. When he returned to the car, the dog had jumped into the front passenger seat and growled when asked to return to the rear of the car. The driver gave in and let her stay where she was. The pie and drink were placed on the central console and the journey resumed. Presently, the driver reached for his pie, only to have the dog's teeth sink into his hand. The dog would not let go, the car was going at 80 miles an hour, the bite was excruciating. Fortunately the driver was able to pull over safely on to the hard shoulder where he eventually talked the dog into letting him go, although he had to relinquish the pie. An incident like this is unforgiveable and could easily spoil a beautiful friendship.

My granddaughter with my pack. These dogs have been taught from the beginning to be calm and to observe the social graces, such as not jumping up or nipping in play. By nature they are not aggressive, but I would not allow a child they did not know to be alone with them. Even with careful training and conditioning, a dog is still a dog and we cannot predict when instinct will surface. For example, a child could accidentally step on a dog's foot, which could make the dog snap in self-defence. Humans do not have fur to protect their skin from serious injury in such an instance.

for a dog to bark a warning, but to threaten or attack a person or dog is not acceptable. It is not a gundog's job to guard, so at the first hint that your dog is taking on that responsibility, you must 'come down hard' on him and leave him in no doubt that guarding is not part of his remit.

What I mean by 'come down hard' is that at the first sign of trouble, you must immediately take hold of your dog's scruff or collar, rate him crossly and push him firmly downwards. Apply the muzzle-holding technique and keep the dog still until he shows acceptance of your authority. Continue to exert the muzzle-hold for several seconds after you stop scolding him, and then slowly let him go. A dog that is just 'trying it on' may need no more than this and will quickly relax and show the whites of his eyes. He will defer to you thereafter.

However, the truly aggressive dog will continue to growl and remain tense while and after you scold him, and when you release him he may attempt to renew the attack. He may even go for you!

Dogs are so quick, and an attack has often already happened before the owner can move to stop it. Thus a scrap is well underway and it is then a matter of separating

the dogs without being bitten yourself. If the dog that is being attacked is on the ground, you can usually pull the attacker off by the collar or scruff, drag him away and then give him a severe trouncing. This may impress the softer type of dog, but it is not a thorough cure in the case of the seasoned fighter; it just gives some satisfaction to the owner of the victim.

Another problem may present itself as you pull the aggressor off, namely that the victim may become emboldened by his apparent magic power in making his attacker suddenly stop. He may then leap up and attack. Therefore, if someone can take hold of the victim as you haul the aggressor away, so much the better. This can prevent you or another human from being bitten.

Castration can be very effective in stopping aggression in a dog, particularly if done when he has only just begun showing the behaviour and before it has become an ingrained habit. Spaying (neutering) an aggressive bitch will usually reduce or remove the trait from her character.

A common cause of a one-sided attack is nervousness. The dog is approached by another creature – it could be human or canine, a cow or a horse – and fear causes him

In a dog fight, the object of the aggressor is to put the victim on his back and bite him on the face and neck. The front legs are also commonly targeted.

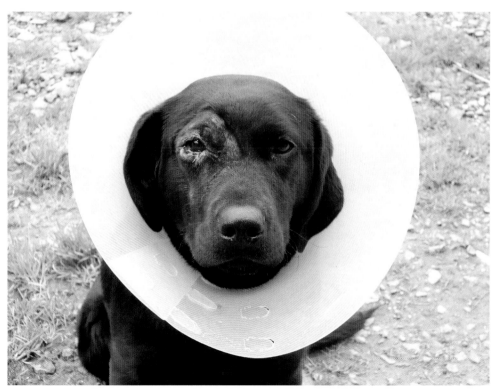

The result of a scrap between two dogs: several stitches and a large vet's bill.

Self-Defence

A Springer Spaniel with a very gentle and obliging nature came to me for a refresher. He liked being with humans and really enjoyed working as a partner with whoever was handling him. He had been brought to me by the kindest of owners, who had acquired him as a young adult from a person known for his harsh handling. As long as things went well, the dog was a complete pleasure, but as with us all, he had his faults, and if you scolded him and went towards him threateningly, he would sometimes show his teeth. I am certain that this was not out of aggression but purely in self-defence so I modified my approach. I was far less confrontational, and he responded with his usual good nature.

You have to be able to let a dog know when his behaviour is not correct, but the approach has to be different for every dog – you need to know your dog. The most suitable correction for this dog proved to be a quiet but stern voice accompanied by a small shake of the scruff, followed by the muzzle-hold, remembering not to stare him in the face.

aggressor sees as his personal space. It could be that a bitch objects to being sniffed by a dog in a personal way, and in this case I agree with the bitch! When two male dogs are involved, it is probably an issue about who is the superior dog. Again, the handlers should intervene before a fight starts, if possible, and *both* dogs should be put on the lead. They should be taken away from each other, and ideally they should then be put where they cannot see each other. This should reduce their adrenalin levels.

However, as a rule there is little warning before a fight develops, and a human who tries to intervene will usually be bitten in the fray. If you can throw a bucket of water over the fighters, this should cause surprise and break up the fight, but then the handlers need to be very quick and grab their respective dogs, taking them off in opposite directions, or the battle will quickly resume. Possibly a hose might do the trick, or covering one dog's head with a large coat, but you still need two people to part the dogs. There is no easy answer if two dogs have begun fighting and are both bent on winning. Just try not to be bitten yourself.

In 1990 I went to The Paris Show, a vast agricultural and food exhibition. We walked around all the animal stalls and I commented on how gentle and kind the horses were. My friend said, 'Of course they are. The French eat all the nasty-tempered ones!'

Aggression in the Home Pack

When a new dog is introduced to your home and your resident dogs, it is important to start off on the right foot. If the new dog is a puppy he will need feeding more frequently than an adult, so to help ward off any jealousy from the adults in your pack, each time the puppy is fed, you should give the other dogs an edible treat. Feed the puppy first and then treat the adults. To do things in this order is to show the older dogs that you hold the youngster in high esteem, so they should too. To give them food whenever the pup is fed also shows them that the presence of the puppy is good news.

If the newcomer is an adult, things can be trickier. Take all possible steps to avoid trouble. If the new dog is bitten by a resident dog, or vice versa, the victim may remain anxious and defensive for a long time.

When a new dog first arrives, he should be put in a kennel or crate where he can smell and hear the resident dogs. About ten minutes after his arrival, allow the other dogs to come and congregate at his door to sniff him through the wire. He can sniff them too, of course.

to snap or bite, thinking that attack is the best form of defence. A visit to the veterinary surgeon can sometimes cause an anxious dog to bite. A muzzle will prevent this, but the dog may need to have his mouth or teeth checked! I refer you to the section on nervousness for your best course of action. The muzzle-holding technique is very effective in these cases as it establishes the idea in the dog's mind that he is under your protection.

An otherwise gentle and kind dog may show his teeth if he is handled harshly. He may even bite in self-defence. When a dog is disobedient, you need to be able to let him know you are not pleased, but it is all in degree – you need to understand your dog. By being less confrontational and using a quiet but stern voice, such a dog should become fully cooperative.

Another common trigger of a fight is when a creature – it could be a human or animal – invades what the

Feeding a puppy in front of a resident dog under your supervision shows the older dog that you hold the pup in some esteem. Therefore, so should he. Giving the older dog a titbit while the pup is eating should make him think the youngster is good news.

This pup is in a cage so that she cannot jump about while the car is in motion, neither can she annoy her elders and perhaps receive a nip of reprimand. Nor can she jump out of the vehicle as soon as the tailgate is opened.

Next, encourage the loose dogs to come with you out-doors so the newcomer can hear them running about and having fun.

It is a good idea to carry a stick when exercising dogs, not because you are lame or to beat them with, but as an aid should any disagreements occur. It is important to maintain an aloof and masterful bearing so that the dogs know you are in charge.

After all the dogs have been shut back in, bring the new dog out on the lead. Have a few quiet words with him and apply the muzzle-hold, just to establish your author-ity. Walk him up and down in front of the others briefly and if he growls you should admonish him and apply the muzzle-hold. Growling from resident dogs should be met with a splash of water. Take the newcomer into the garden on a lead so he can acquaint himself with the territory and spend his pennies if he wishes. After this, put him back in his kennel for about an hour. The next time you go to the kennel, let all the dogs out, new dog last – still on lead – and take them outdoors. The new dog will feel outnumbered and you will probably not have any growling. If there is, tell off the growler without delay, perhaps giving him a tap with your stick. A water pistol can work well too.

Later you could take all the dogs for a short walk, includ-ing the new one, still on lead of course. The fun of the out-ing will defuse any starchiness in the resident dogs and the new dog will soon find their enjoyment infectious. Quite soon he can be allowed to run free with them. If your prop-erty is not dog-proof, you may have to keep the newcomer on lead for several days to prevent any escape attempt, but he will usually become used to the new regime very quickly.

In your home, you should not leave a new dog unsu-pervised with resident dogs until you are certain they are friendly and settled. You may need to keep the new dog in a cage for the first week or so; this will prevent any fights when you are not around, but will still allow the dogs to be together. It will also prevent the newcomer damaging your property out of anxiety.

At the very beginning, allow house dogs to meet the new dog outdoors, preferably on neutral territory. Take them for a walk together for perhaps half an hour. If you have to travel by car, always let the new dog enter the car before the other dogs. He is not likely to guard a car that is not his, and the other dogs should respect your decision, namely that you have allowed him the privilege of going in first. Should a scrap break out, make all the dogs come out of the car, apply the muzzle hold to each in turn, starting with the most uppity. Stand there for

The Victim Type

Occasionally you will come across a dog that other dogs tend to attack for no apparent reason. I once bought an adult Labrador that was a great gamefinder, good-looking, athletic and polite. In addition, he was a field trial win-ner. He was very sweet-natured with dogs and humans, but he was often attacked by other males. I never found out why. Perhaps he said rude things to them under his breath or maybe he just had bad breath! I couldn't even see it coming – all of a sudden, someone had pitched into him; he didn't even fight back! As the scars were beginning to make him look like a pit bull, I sold him to a home where he would be the only dog, together with an explanation as to why I was parting with him. This problem was probably the reason why he had been availa-ble when I bought him, but the vendor did not mention it to me. Caveat emptor!

a minute or so, and when all of them seem calm, begin putting them into the car again. Do not give up. Persist with this method until the dogs submit to your wishes.

At mealtime, feed the new dog first in order to show the others that he is important to you.

OVERDEVELOPED GUARDING INSTINCT

The instinct to guard is not usually strong in our gundog breeds although it is natural for a dog to bark a warning to his owners when visitors arrive or someone comes close to a car he is in. However, he should cease on command. When a dog does more than sound a warning and goes to nip or bite, I consider this to be unacceptable. So does the law. This behaviour must be eliminated promptly. The jaws of a dog are amazingly strong, and a few bites can mean hospital for the victim.

If a dog guards his bed, cage or kennel, you may cure it to the extent that he will not attack *you*, but you will never be able to trust the dog with other people or ani-mals. You must make sure that the dog cannot bite a child or another dog or pet. This dog is a liability and should be discarded. He is not suitable as a gundog.

It should go without saying that you should know where your dog is at all times. If you cannot give him your undivided attention, he should be in a kennel or in the house. Your gates should fasten securely and there should be a sign asking that they are shut carefully.

The very first time you see that your dog is in attack mode, you must act quickly and decisively to prevent anyone from being bitten. You will already have had your suspicions about this dog and so you should be prepared for trouble. Have leads and sticks strategically placed so that you can quickly bring the dog under control. If possible, you should place yourself between the dog and the object of his attention, face him, and quietly but firmly tell him to sit. Scold him if he ignores you but do not shout – that can make things worse. Put a lead on him. You must be determined and definite in your demeanour. If you do not succeed in gaining his submission to you, you must seriously consider parting with him. He is not suitable as a shooting companion. He is not suitable as a family pet. He is a danger and a liability.

ATTENTION DEFICIENCY

Attention deficiency can have a health cause. I have found that a dog carrying a heavy burden of worms, fleas or other parasites often has difficulty in concentrating on his handler. It is a simple matter to deal with this problem – ask your veterinary surgeon for advice.

Attention deficiency can also be due to the dog's nature. Some dogs just seem to find it difficult to concentrate. Often the reason is simply that the dog is still too young for serious training. It may be wise to postpone any formal training for a week or a month, but always insist on basic social graces. I find that at some point there comes a pivotal moment when, out of the blue, the dog looks at you and appears to be saying, 'I'd like to do something interesting with you today.' Try not to miss this moment.

The dog that does not seem to want to please you or pay attention can be very exasperating, but losing your temper will not help matters. If you set such a dog very simple targets, and try to make lessons fun, I think you will find that success breeds success. Err on the side of caution and attempt less than you think the dog can manage. Be very extravagant with your praise and generous with treats. You may find that your dog responds well to your enthusiasm and will try harder. Once he begins to make progress, he will see the point and start to enjoy learning. It is to be hoped that his learning will gather speed and the problem will become a thing of the past. Keeping a diary can be surprisingly encouraging.

DISLIKE OF BEING TOUCHED

Some dogs do not like humans to touch them, especially on top of the head. This can be due to not having been handled enough as a puppy. Puppies should be handled as much as possible. Turn your pup on his back and stroke his tummy. Look in the ears and eyes, push up his lips and check his teeth, hold his paws and separate the toes. This is preparation for when he needs his nails clipped or when you need to inspect his feet for thorns or cuts. He should allow you to hold his tail and lift it up. This will be helpful if you ever need to take his temperature. Be gentle, but persevere.

In the older dog, I believe that a dislike of being touched can be a dominance issue: the dog thinks he is too superior to be touched, especially above his eye level. You must make him understand that he is lower in rank than you or you may find him quite difficult to train. He will question almost everything you try to teach him.

The use of the muzzle-holding technique will go a long way towards making him more cooperative.

You should make him accept your physical attention because it is *our way* of showing when we are pleased with a dog. You can even reward him with treats for accepting your pats and stroking. These hand touches become our tool to tell a dog when he is right. His acceptance of touch also shows acceptance of our leadership. Persevere and eventually he will give in and start to enjoy your touch.

One of a dog's favourite things is to have his ears fondled. If you run your fingers from the base of his ear down the side of the head, you will feel the cartilage of the ear canal. If you gently fondle or squeeze this, most dogs find it delightful. Occasionally a dog may object and squeal: this can be due to an infection in the ear. Consult your veterinary surgeon.

EATING OR ROLLING IN DUNG AND CARRION

Eating or rolling in dung and carrion is a natural thing for a dog to do and is therefore hard to cure. It is extremely

This dog is avoiding being touched on the head, but I believe it is important that a dog allows itself to be handled all over. Acceptance of human touch has many applications – at the vet's surgery, for instance, or to allow the handler to give the dog a stroke to praise him when an exercise has been done well.

Using a treat to persuade a dog that your touch is worth tolerating can help make the dog accept or even enjoy being touched.

Being a Labrador, food works wonders! She has decided that she can bear it for a biscuit.

objectionable if it happens on a shoot day. Not only is it difficult to avoid the dog brushing against you, but he will take the disgusting smell and maybe muck into your vehicle. If he eats carrion or manure, he will often vomit it up – not pleasant in the car or on the living-room carpet. Keep a sharp eye, and insist on good discipline when these temptations are present. Be quick to say 'Leave!' sincerely for showing any interest in them.

Eradicating an Instinctive Leaning

Vigilance and frequent repetition is vital to eradicate an instinctive leaning. One August I was in Scotland with some friends for a few weeks' picking-up on the grouse moors. There was a plague of rabbits at the time on the lower ground near our lodgings, and many of them had myxomatosis. We were given permission to shoot as many as we liked. Everywhere we went with the dogs, we found rabbits in every stage of life and death. There were baby rabbits, teenage rabbits, adults and old ones; fresh dead rabbits, decomposing rabbits, and crispy, dried-out rabbits. The dogs could have made themselves very sick indeed, aside from becoming unsteady on the live ones. They also smelled revolting if they managed to roll in a rotting carcass.

So we spent most evenings, after being on the hill, walking-up in line, dogs at heel and a few of us with shotguns. We were ultra-strict regarding discipline, and quick to tell off our dogs for showing any interest in rabbits, whatever their age or stage of decomposition. We used the command 'Leave!' a lot! Of course this did not apply to the retrieve, and the dogs quickly learned what was allowed and what was not. After four days, none of the dogs showed any tendency to chase live rabbits or to eat dead ones. The rolling problem was not so easy to eradicate, and a sharp eye had to be maintained at all times!

STOCK CHASING

Chasing livestock is a matter of life and death, in the case of both the stock and the dog. Chasing is fundamental to a dog's nature, and doing so satisfies his deepest instincts. Pigs and horses are seldom troubled by dogs – they stick up for themselves – but we must discourage a dog from setting off after any animals, domestic or wild: chasing is unsteadiness. If your dog chases when you have commanded him not to, it usually means you have no real control over him. Chasing cats should be forbidden – even if you do not like cats, chasing is not acceptable.

Sometimes an owner will say, 'He's only playing,' but the animal being chased does not know that, and the results can be very serious.

If you see your small puppy show the slightest interest in poultry, sheep, cattle or other domestic farm animals, leave him in no doubt that it will not be tolerated. A little slap on the muzzle while the pup is looking towards the animals, coupled with a firm 'Leave!' should get the message across. If that is not enough, put a check chain and lead on him and when he looks at the stock, give him a quick tug along with the word 'Leave!'. The word 'No' is used for everyday matters but 'Leave!' is for things that are absolutely forbidden.

With an older dog that has shown an unhealthy interest in stock, you must take a very tough line. If you use strong correction and are consistent, it is possible that you will be able to control the dog even at a distance. However, if you are not present, the dog will almost certainly revert. Your sessions must take place with several different lots of livestock in several different places.

There are three rules you must stick to:

- The first is that you must never walk straight towards the stock with the dog. If you do, it puts you in hunting mode with him and when you punish him, he will be confused. His understanding would be that you were both on a hunting expedition. There must be no confusion whatsoever. You must take a course that runs parallel to the stock, or obliquely, and at least 20 metres away. With poultry you can be closer to the birds, but never go straight towards them. When you change direction, you must always turn away from the animals.
- The second rule is that you must watch your dog like a hawk. You will be able to see the stock in your peripheral vision, but you must watch your dog carefully so that you perceive the smallest flicker of interest.

This pup is young but he must not look at sheep; acknowledge them, yes, but not stare at them. He should be given a firm command to 'Leave' and be called away to do something else. If he ignores you, you may have to give him a light slap on the muzzle and perhaps you will have to put a lead on him to take him away.

The cat is not concerned by the dog's attention, and I don't believe the dog on two legs has any malice in mind. However, I don't like a dog to show real interest in cats as it can lead to chasing, and that leads to unsteadiness.

The instant you see him prick his ears, you must 'go for him'.

- The third rule is that you must not 'pussy-foot' around – you really have to upset him. He should be wearing a check chain with a soft lead. Give a series of three or four sharp jerks on the lead while saying 'Leave!' in a very serious tone. You must really impress him. He must come to think that poultry and stock are very bad news as far as he is concerned. If you do your job well, when he perceives that he is in the vicinity of livestock, he will learn to look away as if to say, 'Sheep? I see no sheep. What an interesting cloud formation that is up there.'

It may be best to start with some hens. If they are your own hens, you have an advantage in that you can use them when it suits you, and if, heaven forbid, things go wrong, you have only yourself to answer to. Otherwise you must find a sympathetic farmer who understands the benefit to him of you correcting your dog. Start outside the pen so there is a physical barrier between you and the birds. Walk your dog up and down along the fence, and if he as much as glances towards the hens, immediately jerk the lead and scold him with a sharp 'Leave!'. Follow the three rules.

When you see your dog's attention is focused on you and he is calm, walk him off lead. Eventually you will gauge that it is safe to take him into the pen, on lead. After a few passes you should be able to sit him up and walk a lead's length from him, never taking your eyes off him and correcting him as necessary. If this goes well, end the lesson and put him in his quiet place.

Try to have a lesson every day for three days, moving in different directions or approaching the birds from another angle, but never walking straight towards them. On the second day, sit him and go to the end of the lead and call him to you. He should have his back to the chickens and you can reel him in if he hesitates. Towards the end of the second day's lesson, you should feel confident enough to take the lead off or wrap it around his neck; leave him sitting with his back to the hens, walk a few metres away from him and call him to you. Have a treat ready to give him the moment he reaches you. Then tell him to sit, put the lead on and put him in his quiet place. On the third day, you may feel able to call him to you along a route where he can see the chickens to one side of him but not very close, say, fifteen paces away. If he

deviates towards them in the slightest, rate him severely, move *away* from the birds and call him again. If you move towards him when he is approaching the hens, he will think you are joining him to chase them.

When it comes to sheep or cattle, use the same strategy. Always move parallel to or away from the animals. Keep your attention firmly on the dog. Be really fierce if he even glances their way.

Do not take chances. You must feel sure he is focused on you and not the stock before you remove the lead. Always leave the check chain around his neck so he has the sensation of being under your control. Only remove the lead for a few seconds at a time. Make the training sessions short – about six minutes. Only change things in small ways – do not try to move forwards with a big step. Always put him in his quiet place after a lesson for at least twenty minutes.

Electrified sheep netting can be hugely helpful in the matter of stock chasing, especially with regard to horses. Your dog could be seriously injured or worse if he goes after a horse. With the permission of the stock owner, take your dog for a stroll parallel to the netting, off the lead. When you perceive he has noticed the animals, say 'Hot!' very sharply. He will not know what this means the first time and he will probably go towards the stock and get a shock when he touches the netting. Repeat the word 'Hot!' a few times – he will be upset so make sure he connects the word with his upset. When a dog learns this word in these circumstances, he will seldom need a repeat lesson. Subsequently, when you see him become interested in something harmful, such as a horse, bull or tractor, say 'Hot!' and he will probably give whatever it is a wide berth.

This may work well in most situations, but when something really gets a dog's blood up, it may take more than the word 'Hot!' to dissuade him.

A shock from an electric collar when the dog is moving towards stock will make him think that the animals have caused the discomfort. This can result in a cure if done in several different places with different farm animals. However, most dogs eventually realise that they only receive a shock when wearing the collar, so it, or a replica, may have to be worn at all times. It is vital that the dog is in your sight when the collar is used so that he is never shocked at the wrong moment. The use of electric collars is illegal in some districts so you must ascertain if they are permitted in yours.

CHASING WILD ANIMALS

The problem of chasing wild animals can be handled in much the same way as the previous one. Chasing a wild animal can easily end in your dog being hit by a car on the road. Better by far to cause him meaningful discomfort yourself, in association with his ideas of chasing, than to have him killed, perhaps not instantly, by a vehicle. In addition, you should bear in mind that he could be the cause of an accident where a human is injured or killed.

Until the dog can be relied upon to obey, you must keep him on the lead whenever it is likely that you will encounter the animals he likes to chase. You must also be ready to correct him with sincerity the moment you perceive he is showing an unhealthy interest in those animals.

Many dogs that have been trained early in life not to pay attention to sheep and other stock seem to view deer and even rabbits and hares as fast sheep – not to be chased! See 'Unsteadiness' in Chapter 8.

CHASING VEHICLES

As with stock, the first time you see the dog show the slightest interest in setting off after a vehicle, scold him sincerely and put him in his quiet place for at least twenty minutes. If he knows the word 'Hot!' that may work as well.

If he is a confirmed car chaser, there are two things you can try. You need the help of two friends for both methods, one to drive and the other to take action to upset the dog. Ask the driver to drive by the dog in an otherwise safe place. When the dog gives chase, the driver must stop and the passenger must jump out of the vehicle as quickly as possible, scold the dog and throw a plastic bucket at him. The bucket should not hit the dog – seeing it skid by should be enough to impress him. This method usually works after three occasions, especially if three different vehicles are used in three different places.

The other method is for the passenger to have a large yogurt cup half full of water. When the dog is running alongside, the passenger throws the water in the dog's face. Obviously the dog has to be running on the passenger side. The former method is by far the more effective because it does not matter which side of the car the dog is on and the passenger does not have to be a good shot.

You, the handler, do not have to be involved in either of these treatments, and it is really better that you are not, as the dog will think that the car has caused his discomfort and upset.

HYPERACTIVITY

Hyperactivity is an innate characteristic. A dog with this nature finds it difficult or impossible to settle. He paces constantly if allowed, and circles in his kennel. He is often destructive and noisy.

This temperament trait is not conducive to training as it prevents concentration and hinders the formation of memory. However, there is a great deal a handler can do to damp it down.

Every time you have the dog with you, whether for training or just exercising, start with the muzzle-holding technique and apply it often during the session. When the dog is in the house or garden with you, apply the muzzle-hold as often as you can. Speak calmly in a low voice; you are not scolding or punishing him, you are simply calming him and showing him that you are important in his life. Using the technique twenty times a day would not be excessive. Dogs live in the moment, so it is probable that he will forget that you have used the technique the instant another idea comes into his mind. Therefore you should repeat it over and over. You must persevere; you are trying to create a new state in your dog's mind, and this will not happen overnight.

When he is being hyperactive away from you, go out and apply the hold at the spot where he was when he began his nonsense. You will need to be determined, but you must also remain calm. If you become overwrought, so will the dog, and matters will escalate. Drop your shoulders – this will help you relax. If you feel your nerves building up, you must call a halt. Take him to his quiet place and apply the muzzle-hold for several seconds as the last thing you do before you shut him up. Leave him for at least an hour. If he is hyperactive while he is shut up, ignore him. You have shut him up because you are worked up and you still will be, so leave him and go out of earshot until you are calm.

In your training sessions, be measured in your movements and words. You should have a plan in mind, and should stick to it as closely as possible. If things go awry, do something you know he understands, and finish for the day. You should underestimate the dog's capabilities, and the tasks you set should be simple and easily achievable for him. In this way you will gain success. You can build on success; you cannot build on failure.

With this type of dog, it will be the work of his lifetime to hold his attention. It is a very frustrating business and unless the dog has exceptional talent, it will be hard for you to persevere. He may never come right and time is precious. He may be happier in a home where less is expected of him.

Neutering the hyperactive dog may effect a great improvement in his behaviour.

OVER-EXCITABILITY

You may think there is little or no difference between this behaviour and hyperactivity, and in some cases you would be right. I believe that many dogs are born with an excitable nature, but that it can also be a learned behaviour.

Certain very enthusiastic dogs can 'boil over' with excitement at the smallest amount of attention from humans, and sometimes from other animals. They jump all over the person or animal, licking and nipping, completely out of control. Sometimes they will spin around in front of, beside, over and under the object of their excitement. Their ability to concentrate on any form of training is practically nil and will not improve until the handler manages to gain some focus from the dog. This behaviour usually shows early on in the way a puppy behaves when he is trying to get attention from, or ingratiate himself to a senior animal. In a puppy it is easy to manage, but when this excitement continues to be exhibited in a grown animal it is not funny. A full-grown Labrador can weigh up to 40kg, and to have that thrashing around uncontrollably is downright dangerous!

Some trainers are reluctant to curb this excitability as they think they may take away some of the dog's keenness to work, or they worry that the dog may become too submissive. The result of ignoring a dog's ruffian behaviour is that later on you may need to be quite harsh in its training. Teaching a dog good manners and respect for people and other animals does not detract from its drive or enthusiasm. In the wild pack a dog would not

be tolerated if it displayed delinquent behaviour, but as a well-behaved and accepted member it would still give of its best in the hunt, and in the protection and welfare of the pack. In our home, an older dog may not retaliate when a youngster becomes over-excited and is rough and very annoying. In such cases you will need to step in, and impress on the pup that his behaviour is unacceptable.

Again, it is an either/or matter: either the dog fits in politely, or he finds that his conduct results in physical unpleasantness.

The first thing you must achieve is control of yourself. The more excitable, hot and fast the dog is, the calmer, cooler and slower you need to be. Dogs mirror our mood and if you become worked up, it will make the dog wilder and more unstable.

This type of dog should always wear a flat, buckle-on type of collar so that you can take hold of him quickly. The collar should fit snugly so he cannot pull his head out of it. When he is behaving like a lunatic, the collar will enable you to hold him still and apply the muzzle-hold to calm him.

If he is charging about in a frenzy and you are unable to catch him, you should remove yourself and any other being that is exciting him, and give him 'time out'. Shut the door on him and leave him completely alone. If he becomes quiet when left alone, you can go back to him after a few minutes with a treat in your hand, and with luck, you will be able to take hold of the collar. Tie a cord about a metre and a half long to the collar so that another time it will be easier to catch him.

When you have hold of him, put him in his quiet place and leave him until he has had time for the adrenalin in his system to dissipate and his pulse rate has slowed. It may take only a few minutes for him to calm down but if he starts barking – and this is quite likely – he will not become calm. Then you must treat his behaviour as naughtiness and follow the advice in the section in Chapter 6, 'Unnecessary Barking or Howling'.

This type of dog should be on lead most of the time, even for exercise. Always insist that he behaves with good manners. Use an extending lead when you are not training. This will help to transfer your calmness to him. Keep the lead on even when you are practising the retrieve so that you maintain control. If you give him freedom before he is reliably obedient, he may revert to the hysterical creature he was.

Your aim is to win this dog's focus. You cannot train without it. Be generous with your praise and treats. Be quick and meaningful with your correction. Stick to simple exercises to give him confidence. Sessions should last no more than six minutes. If you stick with this regime and do not rush into trying to work him free of the lead, he will eventually start to calm himself, begin to associate self-discipline with the reward of training, and start to comply with your wishes.

HYPERSEXUALITY

The problem of hypersexuality is also innate. It is part of the dog's make-up, and something he cannot help. You can punish him, but he will just learn to go out of sight or out of reach in order to pursue his yearning. He cannot curb his feelings, and training him will be difficult and exasperating. He will search constantly for bitches, travelling miles from home; he will cock his leg constantly and will often start fights. He will try to mount bitches whether in season or not. He will try to mount a male dog if there are no bitches around, and this can lead to a fight. He will 'hump' human legs and knock small children down with his attempts at sex. Some dogs 'hump' cushions and their toys. Fond owners may say it is just a case of his being bored or playful, but they are kidding themselves. It is a problem that needs to be addressed. I do not believe it can be overcome through training. In my opinion, veterinary intervention – by which I mean neutering – is the only solution. In addition, management must play a part. The handler must do what he can to avoid the dog becoming bored, and he must be vigilant, and physically correct any signs of unwanted sexual activity.

Hypersexuality occurs in bitches too, though it usually shows in masculine behaviour. They will attempt to mount other bitches when they are not in season. This can lead to a fight. However, if one or both bitches are in season, then mounting is normal and you can ignore it. If a bitch in season accepts the mounting, you can be confident that she will be ready for mating in about two days. This can be very useful to know if you are hoping to have her covered that season. Occasionally, hypersexuality in bitches is caused by a hormone imbalance. Spaying (neutering) will usually work for the good.

In some cases, and in both sexes, mounting is a demonstration of dominance and often occurs in puppies' games. However, if a male dog exhibits hypersexuality at around seven or eight months of age, it would be as well to have him neutered without delay in order to prevent this behaviour becoming an ingrained habit.

Hypersexuality is considered by some to be an inherited trait, so breeding from such a dog is not advisable. If you do not wish to have your dog castrated, you can ask your veterinary surgeon about 'chemical castration', which is given by injection and temporarily removes a male dog's libido, making him more tractable.

GUN NERVOUSNESS

A sensitive nature can lead to gun nervousness in some dogs. It is not the same as gunshyness. The latter is a serious problem and few dogs get over it. It causes them to bolt and hide, and can have tragic consequences. Many gun-nervous dogs recover and become useful workers.

This problem is usually caused by careless introduction of the gun and gunfire. Clients have told me they have taken their youngster out with the gun and fired it 'to see if the dog was gunshy'. This is extremely unwise. You might get away with it, but equally you may frighten the dog for life.

Many dogs are frightened when they first hear a dummy launcher fired, but will tolerate the report of a shotgun. It is generally believed that this is because the sound of the .22 blank used in the launcher is very sharp, whereas the report of a shotgun is in a lower register and not such a crack.

Introduce your dog to the report of the gun or launcher at a distance of, say, 50 metres. As soon as he hears the sound, he should be given a treat, or a dummy can be thrown for him to retrieve. He receives a reward for putting up with the noise. Gradually the distance from the gun can be reduced. The company of a confident dog will help greatly.

An anxious dog will eventually accept anything that he sees every day if he is not hurt or startled in any way. Carrying a gun over your arm, or even a stick, whenever you are with him should do the trick. After a few days you should be able to slowly mount the gun, or stick, as

CASE STUDY: Gun Nervousness – 'Amber' – Cause and Cure

Some years ago, Amber, a well-bred Labrador bitch aged ten months, was brought to me for training. We progressed well and each month her owner came to visit. I like owners to visit for three reasons. First, they maintain contact with their dog. Second, they learn how I teach the dog, how I blow the whistle, manage the retrieve, and so on. Third, they can see if what I am doing is what they want. On the third visit of Amber's owner, she asked if I had introduced the dog to gunfire. 'No,' I replied, 'but we can do it while you are here and it would be a help to have you present.' I gave the lady a handful of biscuits and asked her to give one to her dog the instant she heard the report of the gun. I fetched my .410 and a couple of cartridges, and placed myself about 50 metres downwind of them.

As I raised the gun to fire it into the air, the dog darted behind her owner's skirt, obviously frightened. I did not fire. I walked back with the gun held behind me and asked if the dog had seen a gun before. She confessed that her husband had taken the dog into their walled garden when he was shooting pigeons and the dog had been very frightened by the experience. Imagine how loud the gun would have sounded to a dog in that enclosed space! She said she was worried that the dog had been ruined. I can tell you, so was I!

Armed with this knowledge, I was able to overcome this problem with this dog, but it should never have arisen and we were lucky that the damage was not permanent. I took to carrying my gun most times when we went out for exercise. At other times, I carried a stick about a metre long over my arm to simulate a gun. Amber had to be on the lead for several outings, even when the other dogs were gambolling about around her, enjoying themselves. I began to brandish the gun or stick as if preparing to shoot, at which she would cower – but bribery did work eventually. Gradually I saw that she was relaxed enough to be free, but we remained in a dog-proof enclosure for two or three more weeks. In the kennel I made occasional sudden loud noises, such as dropping a metal food bowl or popping a blown-up paper bag just *before* feeding her. Timing is vitally important – the noise comes first, then the reward for tolerating it.

When I felt it was time to fire a starting pistol for the first time, I asked a friend to help. This would allow me to stand at a distance with Amber on lead while the shot was fired. She was now used to seeing the gun or stick raised but there had been no report. She had been having retrieving lessons, which she thoroughly enjoyed. On the day my friend came to help, I gave him a stick to hold beside the pistol so that it looked more like a gun. He stood 50 metres from us, and on my signal, raised the pistol and stick, and, seeing that she showed no fear, he fired and immediately threw a dummy out to one side. I sent her to retrieve the moment it landed. To our relief, she galloped out, picked it up and brought it to me. It was a fairly short process after that – a matter of a few days – to be able to fire a gun and then gradually move closer with it because she loved retrieving so much. In the end, she became a very good peg dog.

if to fire it, and eventually you will be able to do this at the speed you would when shooting. Gradually you can introduce the bangs as described above.

I usually carry cotton wool with me for the first few outings with a young dog. Then if he shows anxiety at hearing gunfire, I can put a small wad in his ears to deaden the sound. I have found this to be very helpful, but you must remember to take the cotton wool out when you want to work the dog or he may not hear your commands or whistle, or he may not respond because sounds are muffled and therefore different. Or maybe he will just pretend that he cannot hear!

CASE STUDY: 'Punch' and the 12 Bore

I took a one-year-old Cocker Spaniel, Punch, for a couple of days' rabbit training in Northumberland in July. At home he had heard a dummy launcher, a starting pistol and my .410 at a distance and had been unfazed. Up on the rabbit ground, he was happy to hunt and had a very nice pattern. He flushed a big rabbit, his first ever, chased it a few yards but stopped on the whistle. I hunted him on. Suddenly there was a shot from a 12-bore about 20 metres away. I saw Punch cower and he looked very anxious so I quickly asked for a rabbit and put it out for him to retrieve, which he did with alacrity. He hunted on after that, but when he heard the next shot, he came in to heel. He had decided that hunting was causing the bangs and because of the high bracken, he couldn't see the rabbit running or being shot so he wasn't making the connection between the report of the gun and the retrieve. He had decided that coming to heel was the best bet. However, 'bang' goes the gun

'Punch', a Cocker Spaniel who, despite careful introduction to gunfire, was very anxious when first taken out shooting. This was gradually overcome by taking him out with other dogs that had learnt that gunfire means fun.

again so in his mind, being at heel also made the noise happen! So he sat down and would not walk with me. I put the lead on, but even then he was still very reluctant to come along.

After that I found him reluctant to hunt even when he and I were on our own. He came out on the grouse moors where we were a long way from the guns and he was happy to hunt after each drive as long as he was shoulder to shoulder with another dog. On a partridge shoot down south, he became quite relaxed about gunfire at, say, 50 metres, but again would not hunt unless alongside another dog. So it seems he associated the trouble with me. It was quite a challenge, but by taking him out on his own both at home and at shoots we gradually overcame his fears. Eventually he saw that I was connected with the fun and the sport – after all, I'm the one who provides it, I'm the one with the car keys! It wasn't long before he began to enjoy the full pleasure of it all.

GUNSHYNESS

Gunshyness is a problem that is almost always incurable. It is usually innate, but can be learned. I have only known two dogs that were truly gunshy that were cured of it.

Both dogs were so terrified they would bolt for home or some other hiding place if they heard or saw a starting pistol, launcher or shotgun. Both were very well-bred Labradors from a shooting and trialling point of view, so I felt that their introduction to gunfire must have been mishandled.

I was training one of them – a year-old Labrador bitch – for a client. I soon discovered how badly gunshy she was and told the owners there was little hope of making her into a gundog. They took my advice and bought a new pup, keeping the original dog as a pet. In due course the pup came to me for training. She came on well and eventually went home to have many happy days out in the shooting field. Their first dog would be very curious whenever the younger one returned from the shoot and would sniff her all over, obviously noting that the worker had been having a good time. Eventually, the first dog could be taken to a shoot but was left in the car. Presently, however, she showed that she would like to come out and see what was going on. As time went by, she would come out with her companion and presently became a competent picking-up dog, although she preferred to be at a distance from the shooting.

I purchased the second dog for a client who had had several dogs from me previously. She was an eighteen-month-old Labrador called Flair and had reached a good basic standard. The plan was for me to finish her training and introduce her to the shooting field before the client took her on. She came from an experienced trainer, someone I thought I could trust, but obviously I had not taken sufficient care. I should have asked the trainer to show me how she reacted to a gun and gunfire.

It soon became apparent that Flair was terrified of bangs and would run and hide, even if she only saw a gun. For whatever reason, her response to launchers, guns or bangs was absolute dread. She could not go to my client with this problem and I did not have the time to spend on her or the faith that she would come right, so she went to a friend, Sue, to see what she could do with her.

Sue had two other Labradors that were useful picking-up dogs. She decided to carry a deactivated shotgun with her whenever she took the dogs out so that Flair began to associate the sight of a gun with fun but not loud bangs. She had to keep Flair on a lead at first, but in a short while she started to enjoy the outings enough to put up with the weapon. Presently, Sue took the dogs where they could hear shooting in the distance, keeping Flair on the lead. She plied her with treats, which she refused at first, but on seeing the other dogs eating with gusto, she joined in. Over about six months, Flair became steadily more confident out training and within earshot of gunfire. In time Sue was able to take her picking up as long as they were well away from the Guns. Gradually she began to enjoy the retrieving so much that she decided that gunfire was worth tolerating. She eventually became a super picking-up dog.

These two dogs achieved success through different means, but both benefited from the presence of a confident companion dog. In both cases the brave dog showed the scared dog that gunfire equals fun. The other factor was the very gradual and diplomatic reintroduction to guns and gunfire.

HARD MOUTH

Most well-bred gundogs will bring game to their handler undamaged, but hard mouth in some cases is hereditary and therefore innate. You should not breed from a dog with a hard mouth.

Even dogs that start with a soft mouth, and those whose predecessors did not damage game, can become hard-mouthed. There are precautions you can take so that the fault remains dormant and does not come out, whether or not there is a tendency in your dog.

It may seem odd, but hard mouth often occurs in very soft-natured, sensitive dogs. This type of dog does not react well to stress, so if he is put under pressure in a training situation, he becomes tense and the result may be that he takes hold of his retrieves too firmly. You must adjust your approach to each dog you are training to reflect its temperament. Of course, certain rules always apply, such as being consistent, but every dog is different and you need to keep an open mind and respond to each one appropriately.

Too firm handling can cause hard mouth in a tough, brash dog as well, so you can see that you need to be observant in order to detect when a dog feels he is under

---

My Bird or His?

A few years ago, I was walking with the spectators at the Retriever Championships at Windsor and found myself alongside Keith Erlandson, and we got talking. I have always enjoyed his writing and found his methods to be practical and compatible with my way of thinking. I told him about a five-year-old Cocker Spaniel I had that would always bring shot game to hand undamaged, but if he pegged a bird, he would crush it. This puzzled me and I asked Keith if he knew the reason. He said, 'If the game is shot, he considers it is yours, but if he catches an unshot bird, he considers it is his to do with as he pleases.' It sounds anthropomorphic, but who knows. . . I'd like to think he was right.

In order to test for damage to a bird, hold the bird by the neck with one hand and, laying it breast upwards on to your other hand, place your thumb under one wing and the fingers under the other wing, either side of the ribs. Gently massage the body between fingers and thumb. The ribs should feel firm and connected by the spine to the lower parts. If a dog has taken too firm a hold and broken the ribcage and/or backbone, the carcass will almost 'jangle' in your hand.

pressure. The muzzle-hold is very effective in calming a dog and should be used when you see the dog is becoming overwrought or anxious.

Some dogs crush or damage the first few birds they retrieve. This can be because they have not yet learnt how to carry game, or because they are excited. Usually, as they get the hang of it, they bring game gently. Some dogs will crush game when they are working alongside a rival dog. If you can work the jealous dog alone, the problem may disappear.

To check for damage to a bird, hold it on the palm of your hand, its head away from you and the breast upwards. With your thumb on one side of the rib cage and your fingers on the other, feel for damage. If the bird is sound, the ribs will feel firm and intact. If damaged, the carcass will feel as if it is almost 'jangling'.

CHAPTER 6 Problems at Home and Away

A dog with nice manners and gentle social graces is a pleasure to have around. This does not happen by chance: it comes about through training. A dog's natural instincts can make him a nuisance to live with. We need to discourage unwanted behaviour and encourage acceptable behaviour.

Young dogs are usually enthusiastic and optimistic about most things. They adapt easily to a new environment, particularly if it is pleasant and enjoyable. So it follows that if we make a dog's new home a friendly and hospitable place, it will minimise setbacks. We should not spoil the dog, however, by letting him sleep on our bed or feeding him from the table. That will cause trouble for the future. What we must do is give him fair guidelines, good food, exercise, a comfortable, dry bed and kind but firm handling. It is important to start as you mean to go on – to present things to him from the beginning as they will be in the future – but also to give him confidence that you are there to care for him.

It is tempting to feel sorry for a dog that has been taken from all that is familiar to him and brought into a new and strange situation and environment. However, it is important that you treat him with firmness and consistency from the start so that he knows where he stands with you. It is like any other aspect of training – it is a case of 'either/or'. Either he is complying with you and is praised and petted, or he is not pleasing you and is scolded and corrected. Once corrected, he can be praised and petted.

There are dogs that have never been treated with consistency, firmness or kindness, and if you should acquire such a dog, he may blossom under your care, or he may present you with a variety of problems. I give below some difficulties you may encounter, and some ideas that should help to solve them.

It may seem that the problems in this chapter spring from a dog's innate love of attention, and this is often true. They will find all sorts of ways to gain your attention. Beware of dealing with a problem in a way that rewards your dog for doing the wrong thing.

JUMPING UP, LEANING, LICKING AND PAWING

Some dogs love to jump up at or lean against people. This is messy if the dog is wet, muddy or slobbery. It can be dangerous too, especially if the person being jumped at or leaned on is elderly or carrying a gun. Even worse if it is an elderly person with a gun!

Some dogs fuss around you persistently, lick and nip, or strike you in the thigh with a forepaw. Nipping and

This dog is leaning so heavily on his friend that he risks unbalancing him.

This exuberant dog is approaching at speed and the handler knows from previous experience that he has a mind to jump up at her. She swings the hazel stick like a pendulum in front of her.

The swinging stick is a deterrent.

The dog is deflected.

clawing can be very painful – dogs do not realise that our skin is very sensitive. Older people's skin is usually very friable and a scratch can cause profuse bleeding.

Of course, dogs should be discouraged from any of these things when they are very small, but some owners are inclined to be too tolerant with puppies. They think puppies should be 'allowed their puppyhood', by which they mean that the pup may do whatever he likes. This is wrong thinking. Puppies can learn good behaviour as easily as bad. Dogs do not become more intelligent beyond the age of about ten weeks than they ever will be. They become more able, physically and mentally, and their memory improves, but their intelligence does not alter. You should never allow a puppy to do anything that is socially unacceptable. If you do, you will have to correct it later, so nip it in the bud!

We should not wish to discourage shows of affection – after all, the dog is our friend and sporting companion – but there are limits, and preventing a dog from being a

He comes round to sit in front of the handler as a positive alternative, and is praised.

nuisance should not stop him being fond of us. We need to make good behaviour rewarding and bad behaviour unpleasant, physically. Show the puppy or dog that once it has stopped the undesirable behaviour, you are pleased with him and will give him praise and affection. This may trigger the bad behaviour all over again, but if you are determined, and repeat the correction followed by praise as many times as is necessary, the dog should eventually realise what you want. Dogs understand an 'either/ or' world.

If he does not seem to grasp what you mean, you will have to change tactics. Correct the unwanted behaviour and then put the dog in his quiet place for up to half an hour. When he comes out, be friendly, but if he re-offends, put him back in the quiet place. Sooner or later he will understand, but you need to be more determined than he is!

As mentioned earlier, it is a good idea to carry a stick when you are exercising dogs. You can use it to fend off a dog and prevent him from jumping up at you. Hold the top of the stick and place it vertically or at an angle between you and the dog as you see him approach. Also, should you be unlucky enough to trip and fall, dogs are often eager to help and comfort you by rushing up and licking your face, and a stick is a great help in keeping them at bay while you regain your feet!

SNATCHING FOOD

It is very important to cure the bad habit of snatching food immediately it appears, as it can lead to hard mouth.

Dogs snatch food from each other, but when a dog snatches food from his human handler, he does not realise

All dogs should be taught to take things from the hand gently. These two wait politely until the treats are given, and take them without snatching.

Taking a treat nicely; the other dog waits patiently.

that it hurts if he catches our fingers. To prevent him from biting your fingers, enclose the food in your fist and offer him only the back of your hand. Say 'Gently', and as long as he doesn't try to be rough, slowly unfold your hand and turn it over until he can take the food from your palm. If he is rough, knock his muzzle with your closed hand hard enough to make him draw back. As you do this, make a sharp sound as though you are hurt. The dog comes to associate your yelp of pain with the discomfort he feels when you knock him. Repeat the procedure until he shows due respect. Only then should you allow him to have the food. With a particularly bad offender, wearing gardening gloves is a good idea.

NOT SETTLING IN THE KENNEL, HOUSE OR CAR

If your new dog or puppy is noisy and refuses to settle, there are several things you can do to help. Give a puppy about fifteen minutes' exercise so he lets off steam. If it is an adult dog, take him out for half an hour or more so he is comparatively calm.

Your dog's bed should be in a kennel or a cage so he cannot do any damage. Put a towel or something similar that has your scent on it in his bed. Take the pup or dog to his bed and show him the bedding, giving it a little pat and encouraging him to sniff it. Your command is 'In'. Put him in with a bribe, and shut the door of the kennel or cage for a few moments. Some dogs will not take the biscuit because they sense they are not going to like the situation. Whether he eats it or not, open the door and bring him out for about a minute. Do not make a fuss of him when he is out; only praise him when he is in the kennel or cage. Repeat this process twice more.

The fourth time you put him in, say 'Stay' and go out of sight for a very short time – only three or four seconds – your intention is to return before he has made a sound. If he has been quiet, praise him sincerely and bring him out, on the lead if necessary, and go for a short stroll. If he makes the smallest sound when you shut his door and go out of sight, go back saying 'Be quiet' and splash him in the face with a little water. Step out of sight for an instant and then return as a nice person, speak kindly to him and give him a treat, then bring him out.

In this way the dog learns several reassuring things. He can smell your scent in his bed. The door opens so it is not prison. You put him in several times so you meant

it. You let him out so you are not such a bad person after all. The biscuit may now have some appeal. Repeat the procedure at least twice more, each time leaving him for a short while longer. Give him a treat each time he goes in, especially if he goes in without you having to be physical with him.

He also learns that his noise results in being splashed with water. Do not tolerate any noise, even in the first hour. The dog must understand from the outset that noise is forbidden. You should not let him out if he makes a noise – that would be a reward for being noisy. If he goes quiet when you return to splash him, you must still do it or he will think he has trained you to return.

Dealing with a new dog in this manner makes him settle almost straightaway. There is seldom any howling or refusing to eat. Puppies can take longer to accept being shut in, but if you feed him his meals in the cage and always reward him with a treat for going in, he will gradually begin to regard it as his own space. If you have small children, the cage will be his refuge and the children should respect this. Puppies need lots of sleep. He will quickly realise that he is not disturbed when he is in his cage.

Training a dog to settle in the car requires the same treatment as for cage, house or kennel. Only leave him for a few seconds at first, or no time at all if he makes a noise. If he makes the smallest whine or yip, go to him immediately, say 'Be quiet!', and splash him with a little water. Then leave him again. This may take up a lot of your time, but once he has learnt the form, you should not have to go through it again. Some dogs are very destructive when left in the car, so a cage is a valuable item. *See also* 'Unnecessary Barking or Howling' later in the chapter.

CAR SICKNESS

Being in a moving vehicle causes many puppies and dogs to be sick or to drool uncontrollably. However, almost all dogs will stop once they gain a good association with being in a car and travelling. Once they learn that they go to fun places in the car, they usually give it up spontaneously. Try feeding your dog his meals in the car, leaving the door open so that he does not feel like a prisoner. Take him for short trips, always giving him a biscuit when he goes into the car, and have him out for a walk or short training session at the end of the outward journey. This should soon build a nice idea in his mind about what the car means, and he should give up his vomiting and drooling.

If this doesn't work after a few months, ask your veterinary surgeon for help.

REFUSING TO ENTER THE CAR

A dog that has been in an accident will fear entering a vehicle for a long time afterwards, perhaps for life. Many dogs are afraid of getting into the car because they suffer from car sickness, but the problem can also be due to the driver. Sudden hard braking or cornering can result in a dog being thrown about in the vehicle, and this is bound to upset him. A crate does much to limit this, but the driver should be conscious of his passengers and drive considerately. There should be some sort of bedding or matting to prevent a dog from sliding around with the motion of the vehicle, and some kind of padding at the front of the crate to cushion him in the case of an emergency stop.

In curing the dog's reluctance to enter the car, it is best to be firm and quick. Have a flat collar on him and a lead. Bring him to the tailgate and give the command 'In you get!', indicating the lip of the car with a pat of your hand. The dog will hang back. Take the collar in your weaker hand and put your stronger one under his hindquarters and bundle him into the vehicle. If he is too big for you to manage this, enlist the help of someone who can, while you stand on the other side of the dog, giving the command and signal. Immediately he is in the vehicle, offer him a treat and give lavish praise. Whether he takes the treat or not, invite him to get out of the vehicle straightaway. This shows him that entering the vehicle is a good thing and that he is not stuck there.

Repeat this treatment three or four times in the first session, hesitating only a moment before bundling him in. He needs to realise that he does not have a choice, and that as soon as he is in, he will have a reward, lots of praise, and will then be asked to come out. Do not take him for a drive at this stage – put him in his quiet place to think it over. Later in the day you can have another session. Usually after two sessions you will find that as you reach for his collar, he will jump into the car.

When you begin to take him off for a drive, each journey should be short, with fun at the other end. Gradually he will be willing to enter the vehicle without reluctance.

UNNECESSARY BARKING OR HOWLING

I believe any dog should be permitted to bark a warning to his owner if there is a visitor to the property, particularly a stranger. But once the owner says 'Be quiet!' the dog should stop. The command should not be shouted – the dog must not think you are joining in – and you need to time it so you are heard between barks. Howling is tricky because a dog cannot hear you while he is howling unless you are close by.

The simplest and most harmless deterrent to noise-making is a splash of water in the dog's face. You only need a small amount of water – use a water pistol or plastic cup. Inside the house or car, splashing the dog with water may not be very acceptable, although with a water pistol and good aim it may be worth making the sacrifice.

If the dog is in a kennel quite a distance from the house, when you hear barking, start walking towards

The Shoe Trick

Most puppies howl or cry when they first come away from their mother and siblings. This can be very trying, and if you are cross with the pup, it may upset your other dogs. An old farmer friend of mine told me about a collie pup he had when he was a boy. She was kept in the outhouse, and night after night she howled and howled. My friend's mother decided the pup should be left in the kitchen to see if she would settle there. The family went up to bed and not a sound was heard from the pup all night. When they came down in the morning, they found her with her nose and most of her head deep inside a work boot: the comfort of the smell seemed to have calmed and soothed her. I tried this with my latest puppy, using an old training shoe. All was peace and harmony. You may say that this would encourage a pup to take shoes and belongings he should not have, but it's up to us to keep our more precious things out of harm's way.

the kennel, cup of water in hand, saying 'Be quiet!' every few paces in a clear but not loud voice. When you are near enough, splash the dog at least once, then retire. As soon as he begins again you must repeat the process.

Another way is to hook up a hose from a tap at the house running out to the kennel. Fix the spout so that it points at the barker. When barking commences, go to the tap and say 'Be quiet' just loud enough for the dog to hear, and turn the water on for three or four seconds. This will impress the dog quite considerably as it seems that you are at a distance but can still splash him. However, if the dog is howling, he won't be able to hear you, so just turn on the tap and when the howling ceases, say 'Be quiet' in a normal voice.

There will be times when you are staying away from home, perhaps shooting, trialling or working your dog, and you have to leave him in the car. It is very annoying for anyone in earshot if a dog will not remain alone quietly in the vehicle. To achieve this, have him outside the car on a lead, and saying 'Be quiet', splash water in his face in cold blood. Put him in the back of the car with the front window open a crack so he can hear you, then go out of sight. When he begins to bark, say 'Be quiet', and go back and throw water straight at him. Of course it will splash the window and not wet him, but the sight of the water coming at him will usually be enough to do the trick.

Occasionally you will meet a dog that actually enjoys the splash in the face. In this case, a rolled-up newspaper, bound with sticky tape, makes an effective but not harmful deterrent. In cold blood, with your dog on a short lead, face him and say 'Be quiet' and give him a sharp tap on the side of his muzzle or neck with the rolled-up newspaper. Repeat this a few times, then put him in his quiet place for an hour.

The next time he starts barking, say 'Be quiet' and brandish the rolled-up newspaper. You may not even have to use it. However, if he ignores you, give him a sharp tap and shut him in another room. If he carries on barking, go to him and if he is loose, give him one tap, then whack the walls and floor near him, meanwhile repeating 'Be quiet' in a firm but quiet voice. This will usually upset him enough to make him obey you. If he is in a cage, knock the cage two or three times with the paper.

If he is out in a kennel, say 'Be quiet', just loud enough for him to hear you. If he continues to bark, you must hurry out to him saying 'Be quiet' and whack the paper against your leg as you go. When you reach him, show him the paper, which may be all you need to do. If he persists in barking, whack the paper against the wire of his run. He should be quite upset and will perhaps go into his bed, and if this is his reaction, praise him, and as you leave say 'Be quiet' and 'Stay'.

On the other hand, if he is loose in the garden, and he still defies you after being shown the paper, it is tricky as he is unlikely to let you catch him. Just follow him at a steady walk, saying 'Be quiet' and eventually he should lower his tail and perhaps go indoors. Change into a friendly person and put him in his quiet place. Before you let him out again, tie a cord to his collar so that you can catch him next time.

PICKING UP STONES OR STICKS

Retrieving dogs like nothing better than to have something to carry, but some things can be dangerous. Often when a dog is first let out for exercise he will pick up stones or sticks in excitement. The worry is that he may swallow the item. Try your best to remain calm, call him to you and gently take the object. Hold him by the collar or put him on lead, and keep him beside you until he calms down or you can offer him something else to interest him, such as a toy. You could bring the dog out of the house or kennel with something already in his mouth, a toy or bone, for example. Or you can have him on lead and do some simple training exercises before you let him free.

You will have to do this repeatedly each and every time you bring the dog outdoors for many days. It may take weeks for you to break this behaviour if it has become a habit. Sometimes moving the dog to another kennel or taking him out by another door will bring about a change.

You should not let your dog think you like him to carry sticks, even though it might be a handy log for the fire. He may develop the idea that when you send him for a retrieve and he cannot immediately find it, a stick or log will do instead. When he brings you something you don't want him to have, take it from him gently but with no praise, then when he is not looking, hide it where he cannot reach it.

Disturbing Gift

One day my Golden Retriever, Pearl, proudly brought me a skinning knife with only the handle showing outside the front of her mouth. The blade was a handspan long and was inside her mouth, so the tip must have been at the top end of her tongue! It was extremely difficult to remain calm, but there was no alternative: to shout and run at the dog might have ended in disaster. I had to master my panic and thank her for bringing it, and take it as gently as I could.

'Pearl', a Golden Retriever – she is very happy to retrieve anything, even a skinning knife!

CHAPTER 7 Dog Gone!

RUNNING OFF, CHASING AND HUNTING FOR HIMSELF

In my opinion, running off is the worst and most worrying of all problems in dogs of any kind. In a gundog this behaviour shows a lack of cooperation between dog and handler, and a void where there should be team spirit.

Most of us have seen that look, the look that means that the dog has switched off from his owner and is on a mission to follow a scent or chase another animal or bird. It is a look that can fill you with despair, because as a human, you have little or no chance of keeping up with a dog, let alone catching him. You may have a warning – he may gaze into the distance for a few seconds – but then he is off! You know you have lost communication with him: he is in a world of his own, and you have little or no chance of regaining contact with him until he decides to return.

Your imagination goes into overdrive, and you picture any number of horrific happenings. A farmer or gamekeeper may see him and decide he is endangering their stock or birds, and as a last resort, they have a legal right to shoot your dog. A car may run him over, and perhaps he will not be the only one to suffer in the collision. He may fall over a cliff or be caught up in wire. You may never see him again, never know what happened to him. However, you must remain calm so that you can handle matters sensibly. It may help if you remember that most dogs return to the last place they were with you.

To succeed in curing this fault, you must address it without delay. You must be determined and consistent, and must maintain a positive attitude. You may also need to be quite severe with the dog. You may feel that you do not have it in you to be harsh with your dog, but to break this habit, desperate measures may be needed. There is an anger that arises from the fear of danger to one dear to you. Would this anger enable you to be really tough on your dog? If you do not cure the problem he will have to be kept on a lead for life. This is in no way practical for a working gundog.

Certain dogs seem not to care if they are with you or not. This is not promising, as your gundog should be a cooperative companion. This type of dog may not respond to retraining.

Choose a new command and whistle signal that mean absolutely what you want. You must erase the old sounds from your repertoire. Keep him on a long line and use it to reel him in every time you call him – quite soon, the dog should turn and come of his own accord. Remember to praise him sincerely.

When he is reliable to your call while on the line, take him into a small pen about the size of half a tennis court. After calling him to you a few times on the long line, let him loose. Only call him when he is in the same radius as he was on the long line. Insist on instant obedience to the command or whistle. If he is slow to obey, scold him sincerely and put him back on the line. Do not be proud – it is not an admission of failure to put the line back on, it just means that the dog has not yet 'got the message'. Keep practising, sometimes free and sometimes on the line. When he is reliably obedient in that pen, take him to a larger enclosure to practise, making sure that he obeys instantly, then graduate to another enclosure, and so on. The reason for practising in different places is to teach the dog that he must obey everywhere, not just in one place. The reason for the enclosure is that he will be under some degree of control and not able to run completely free. Bribery will help with most dogs.

Do not do the exercise in more than one pen in a session – a dog needs time to absorb a lesson. I often think we go too quickly from one thing to the next for dogs to assimilate what we are trying to convey.

There should be no distinction in your mind between walks and training sessions. To a dog, every outing is a learning opportunity. You should be aware of your dog's body language at all times. Call him frequently. He should come and remain with you until you give your release command. If he comes but immediately wants to rush off, detain him – physically – until you have given the release command. Every so often, put the lead on for a short while, then release him. If you only put the lead on when the outing is over it will signal the end of his fun. You should be showing him that you provide fun by releasing him often and by taking him to new places.

Off lead he may refuse to respond instantly. After you blow the whistle, let it fall from your mouth – you must not keep blowing as it will become just a location device for your dog. Move away from him rather than towards him. This should make him think you are willing to abandon him if he doesn't come. He may also think you have something more interesting to investigate in your direction than he did in his. Going towards the dog can make him think that you are joining him in the fun, particularly if he has begun to chase something. If he is heading towards danger, seeing you running in the opposite direction may make him turn away from it. If he does not come after you, give one more call and then hide where he cannot see you, but where, if possible, you can see him. Presently he should come to look for you – hopefully in a bit of a panic. He may not see you and may charge past, in which case call him in a reassuring voice and give him lots of praise when he reaches you. He should be very relieved to find you.

Desperate Times Call for Desperate Measures

I once had a spaniel that very much liked to suit herself. She would go off without a backward glance and was deaf to the recall. She would eventually return to look for me, but when she saw me she would say, 'Oh, there you are. See you later!' and be off again. After trying to reteach her by the methods described above without success, I decided that a more serious approach was needed. I was loath to be harsh with her, but she was putting herself in danger.

A friend and I devised a plan. My dog did not know my friend very well. I was lucky enough to have the use of two-way radios. There was a particular place where this dog had run off on several previous occasions. It was in thick woodland with one main path that led to a more open, tussocky area where she could amuse herself hunting for birds and rabbits for quite some time. Leaving the dog in the vehicle, I equipped my accomplice with a rolled-up newspaper and took him to a spot near the far end of the path before it opened out on to her hunting ground. He would be positioned about 150 metres from where I would be. I gave him some instructions and asked him to wait out of sight.

I returned to the car and brought the spaniel out on the lead. We did a few minutes of obedience training and recall on the lead, and then I let her off the lead. We then started off down the path. I gave her the release command and off she darted. When she had gone a few bounds, I blew the recall whistle. As expected, she ignored it. I spoke to my friend on the radio to say she was on her way. He was able to see her approaching, and as she came to within 20 metres of his position, he leapt out into her path, brandishing the newspaper and slapping it on his free hand and roaring at her. Hearing this, I blew the recall signal and the dog turned in her tracks and came straight back to me. I made her understand that I was delighted with her, petting her and giving her treats.

My friend is very patient and realised the gravity of the situation so he was willing to help me on three or four more occasions in different places. All this turned the tide, and the little spaniel became less disrespectful and more willing to act in partnership with me.

An important point to note about this treatment is that the unpleasantness happened when the dog was 'in the act'. The result was that she returned to me in answer to the whistle and received an ecstatic welcome. There was no doubt about which scenario was preferable to her. She soon realised that when I called her, she had to get herself to the spot from where I had called her as quickly as she could! That dog was never a paragon of virtue, but this treatment made her much more thoughtful and cautious, and it was effective in bringing her back to me ever after without delay.

In It for the Long Haul

A friend had a spaniel that would get 'the look' and then be gone for hours. The worry this caused her was almost unbearable. She was discussing the problem with an elderly friend, and he advised her to attach the dog to her belt with a long line every time they went out, and to do that for six months. This meant that all the fun the dog had was in her company. She decided to give it a try and see it through for the full six months. She did not make a fuss about it, but always pretended to the dog that this was the natural way to be. She continued to train him by word and whistle, and rewarded him with titbits and stroking whilst they were connected to each other. She also did a lot of training in an enclosure where she could have him free but where they both knew she would be able to enforce her commands. She used many different enclosures so he did not have the idea that he only had to behave well in one place. She also had the dog castrated. I think this played a large part in why the treatment worked, which it did.

She now has a companion who is in tune with her, and they enjoy many happy outings together. He has become quite a useful picking-up dog. However, she confessed to me recently that she still sometimes takes him out on the long line, just for the relaxation and peace of mind it gives her when she might be distracted by company or there are a number of alluring distractions for the dog.

When free, your dog should always be in view. If he is a spaniel, do not let him go more than 15 metres from you. A retriever may be allowed a radius of 40 metres, but less if it means he goes out of sight. You would probably exercise dogs of the pointing breeds in open country as they need more scope, but all dogs should have you in their mind all the time when loose.

You must not punish a dog when he eventually returns to the place where you first called him: he must feel confident that being back there with you is a nice place to be. However, if you can go out to him and show him you are displeased when he is where he should *not* be, he will see that as fair. Some dogs are amazed that you will take the trouble to go out to them, which is why you should do just that. It does not matter how long you take to reach him, but you must be prepared to make the effort. It really does impress most dogs.

When you catch up with him away from where he should be, even if he looks sorry, show him that you are cross, put him on the lead, and walk him back to where he should be, then be really nice to him. Praise him sincerely. When you set off again, keep him on the lead and take another direction, which you know will be good fun for him. This is to show him that *you* call the tune, and that if he goes where you choose, it will be interesting and enjoyable.

Do not take your dog for exercise at the end of the afternoon when it will soon be dusk. This is the time that deer come out from cover to graze. Dogs seem to know this, and the scent of deer seems to carry well. Your dog can become semi-feral in an instant.

I cannot emphasise too strongly that when scolding or correcting a dog, it must be done when the dog is in the wrong. A single moment can make all the difference between the dog learning to do what you want, or learning to fear and mistrust you. This is why you must be ready to change from nasty to nice in a split second.

Breaking the habit of ignoring your recall command or whistle signal will take a lot of time and determination on your part. Always strive to show the dog that it is in his best interests to respond to you, that it is preferable and will lead to praise, treats and a good relationship with you. In time, you should achieve your aim – it will be worth the trouble.

CHAPTER 8 Troubles With Basic Training

If you are told that you should go back to the basics with your dog, you may feel rather affronted. However, if you do it, you will find that it pays off. Whenever you meet stalemate or some hiccup, do not hesitate – go back a stage or several stages. It really does work.

HEELWORK

'Heel' is the position a dog should assume and maintain at his handler's side (always the same side), facing forwards with his handler, his head or shoulder level with the handler's knee, whether standing still or walking.

Good heelwork should begin when you first put a collar and lead on a puppy. He should never be permitted to

This Golden Retriever is walking tidily at heel and is attentive to his handler.

pull or chew on it. Of course you must be very gentle with a young dog, but you can still make it nicer for him to walk on a slack lead than to pull. If you knew your puppy was going to grow into something the size of a horse that weighs upwards of half a tonne you would surely never allow him to begin pulling, would you? I suggested this to a friend who said, 'Actually, there are people who allow their horses to pull them all over the place. Then someone needs to be very fierce indeed to cure them.' Why let the problem develop in the first place?

If heelwork is not taught correctly in the early stages of training your young dog, poor performance may haunt you the whole of his life. Good heelwork is a kind of steadiness and self-discipline on the dog's part whereby he resists any temptation to leave the correct position. If he pulls or deviates from your side in any way you will need to go back to the beginning and reteach him.

Problems with heelwork are very common. Before any corrective training commences, however, you may need to rule out certain things.

Fear of the Lead

Consider the matter like this: a lead or collar is, after all, a noose, and potentially could strangle a creature, and all creatures know this! Therefore the handler must be careful, slow and gentle, and should make the process as pleasant as possible for the dog. Food can play a big part in this and can help speed up the process of solving the problem. All the training must take place indoors or in a safe enclosure until the dog has overcome his fear.

I like to begin with the flat buckle-on sort of collar with a clip-on soft lead. Show the dog the collar and lead and let him mouth it if he wants, but not take it from you. It is yours. Drape it across his neck and body and trail it beside you as you walk about with him. He may not stay near you but he will notice the lead and gradually he will accept its presence. Dangle it near his face when you are about to feed him and when you are about to allow him through doorways. Give him good associations with it. This may take many days but eventually he should see it as a harmless belonging of yours.

Some dogs have had such a frightening experience with a collar and lead that you will have to be very sympathetic indeed. Mealtime is an excellent place to start. Prepare his food on a table or shelf above his head. Teach him to sit for his food by holding the bowl above his head until he sits, then quickly put the food down for him to eat, saying 'Paid for'. At each subsequent meal, try to keep him sitting for a little longer before you put his food down. The longer he has to wait, the keener he should be to eat when you put the food down. When he is quite steady and waits for 'Paid for' you can move to the next stage.

When it is suppertime, place the collar and lead on the floor next to the spot where you usually put his bowl. Let him watch you prepare his food. Tell him to sit. Place the food bowl on the floor near the collar and lead and say 'Paid for' straightaway. Leave the room but stay where you can watch him. When he begins to eat, praise him quietly. Repeat this over the next few days, each time placing the lead at a different angle or distance from the dog.

When the dog seems comfortable to be near the lead, take it in the same hand as the food bowl as you place it on the floor. Say 'Paid for', and trail the lead over the bowl. Go out of the room. If all goes well, he should be happy enough to eat with the lead touching his face. The next day you should be able to lay the lead on the floor between the dog and his bowl so he must step over it to reach his food. The next step is to draw the two ends of the lead into a large loop and hold it so that he must put his head through it to reach his food. The idea is that he must tolerate the lead's touch in order to have his meal. If he puts his head through the loop, slowly lower it until it rests on his neck, and leave him to eat. Each day, as long as he volunteers to put his head through, reduce the size of the loop. In a sense, he is 'paying for' his meal by accepting the lead. While he eats, you should sit nearby, quietly praising him. Call him to you when he has finished eating and remove the lead.

He may take fright at any point, but keep calm and speak kindly to him all the while. You may not make any progress on some days but eventually, if you are not hasty, all will be well.

Spend a few minutes each day sitting on a low seat, feeding him small treats while you accustom him to the collar. Lay the collar across your knees. Try holding it in one hand while he is taking a treat from the other and smooth it against his cheek. From here you may be able to drape it across his neck for a moment, and eventually you should be able to do up the buckle and let him go free wearing the collar. He will probably have a good scratch, shake his head and try to run away from the annoying thing – that is only natural.

Once you have done up the collar do not hold on to it – let him go free. If he will not allow you to undo the buckle he will have to keep the collar on. This may be a good thing, especially if he will still take treats from you or eat his supper while wearing it. Next day, before his breakfast and again before his supper, see if you can attach the lead to the collar but do not hold on to it; just set him free with the lead trailing.

When you do take hold of the lead, do so slowly and carefully and go up to him rather than reeling him in to you. Unclip the lead but leave the collar on. This will make the procedure easier next time. Continue with this method every day until he is completely relaxed about having the lead attached and then detached.

The next stage is to take him outdoors to an enclosure about the size of half a tennis court. Have him on the lead and allow him to sniff and wander at will. Hold the lead as if it were made of cotton, and let go if he is at all bothered. Thus he will realise that he is not permanently restrained. Leave the lead on when he is loose until you feel sure that he will come to you.

A dog with a strong hunting or retrieving instinct will accept the collar and lead quickly if he associates them with going training. As soon as you feel he is relaxed enough, introduce simple retrieves, even though he is still trailing the lead. My dogs push forwards to put their head into the loop as if to say, 'The lead means training – let's go!'

Refusing to Have a Collar or Slip Lead Put On

The commonest cause of a dog refusing to have a collar or slip lead put on is that as soon as the handler puts the lead on, he tightens it. There is no reason for tightening it: it has just become a habit for the handler to do it, and the dog understandably takes a dislike to the lead. You must make yourself conscious of this habit and then break it. You must be mindful at all times of what you are doing at your end of the lead, and do not exert any tension without meaning to.

Teaching a dog to put her head in the loop of the lead freely and willingly. Tell your dog to sit. Have a treat in one hand and the loop of the lead in the other. Hold them in front of the dog and say 'head in'.

Use the treat to entice the dog to put her head through the loop while continuing to say 'head in'.

Give the treat as you draw the lead on to her neck. Be sure not to tighten the lead once it is on the dog; you are trying to build pleasant associations.

Use a treat to entice the dog to put his head through the loop of the lead on the command 'Head in'.

Treats will help a great deal when putting on the buckle type of collar, too.

If you have to take the dog anywhere on the lead during this training phase, don't worry, but just keep the lead slack for as much of the time as you can, use bribery, and make sure that the outing is a happy one, or at least ends happily.

Pulling on the Lead

Pulling on the lead is one of the commonest problems with dogs. Let alone the harm a dog might do to his handler, a dog that pulls on the lead can cause damage to his own windpipe. He can also put sufficient pressure on his legs to cause malformation of the joints.

There is a real danger that a sudden lurch can pull the handler over. If he is lucky, the fall may cause only minor bruising, but to my knowledge, such falls have sometimes resulted in serious injury to the handler. I know people who have suffered broken ribs, punctured lungs, broken wrists, arms and knees.

If pulling is an ingrained habit in your dog, change your command and start afresh. The new command

A dog that constantly pulls on the lead can spoil the outing. It is hard on the handler's joints and the dog's throat.

This is the correct way to tighten the check chain when telling a dog that it has moved out of the correct heel position. The arm away from the dog swings out sideways to give a firm tug but then is loosened immediately. It is intended to cause momentary discomfort, like the quick nip of another dog.

must mean exactly what you want it to mean and your dog should never hear the old command again. Instead of 'Heel' you could change to 'Close' or 'Walk'.

It is important to understand why dogs pull on the lead. They pull because they can. They can because it does not hurt very much. The skin of a dog's neck is very thinly endowed with nerve endings because this area has become insensitive over the thousands of generations of dogs as it is the area where they rag and pull at each other in play fighting. Dogs also pull because they do not realise that they have a choice – they could walk on a loose lead and be comfortable, but they don't know this until they are taught. Dogs pull in order to be out in front. We do not want this, as it means they may be in our way and it allows them to notice things before we might.

Use a check chain and a soft leather or fibre lead. Have your dog sitting beside you and put the collar on correctly and attach the lead. Hold the lead in your strong hand: your dog should be on your other side. That means that if you are right-handed, your dog should be on your left. The lead comes across your body. Your other hand, the one nearest the dog, will be relaxed and empty and will appear to the dog as it will when your dog has been trained to walk nicely at heel. The picture the dog sees is very important to him.

Let us say that you have changed your command to 'Close'. Standing on the spot, say 'Close' and 'Good dog' several times, just to give him the idea that being next to you is the heel position and that it pleases you for him to be there.

The next step is to teach him that 'Close' also applies when you are walking together. As you are about to move forwards, say 'Close' in a quiet, firm voice and begin to walk. If the dog lunges forwards, stop, give the lead

Another method of encouraging a dog to walk to heel. The handler has passed the lead behind her back. This can give more stability to the handler if the dog pulls. In addition, because it shows the dog a new picture, it can help stop the pulling and poor positioning.

It may be that a handler is too frail or elderly to correct a dog that pulls strongly on the lead. This handler employs a Halti to control her dog. It acts as a halter does on a horse; this gives her control of the dog because she has control of its head.

Two playful dogs. The English Setter (right) is wearing a Halti, which gives the handler relatively easy control over severe pulling.

a meaningful tug and at the same instant say 'No!' 'No' means, 'You're wrong and you must not do this!' The lead must only be tightened for a moment. Your arm action should be similar to that used when starting a lawn mower, pull and release, so that the pressure on the dog's neck is sharp but momentary. Your arm should move out to your side, not upwards. It is not a positioning movement, it is a reprimand.

Tailor your tug to the temperament and size of your dog. If he is small or very timid, a quick but not hard tug should be enough. At the other end of the scale, a bold, brash, strong dog may require a bold, strong correction, and you may need to add the strength of your free hand for that correction. In between there are other types of dog. Use only the amount of correction necessary to obtain cooperation. The instant he is in the heel position, you must change into his friend and praise him genuinely.

Sometimes this results in him launching immediately into another pulling spell. Correct him and then praise – you must be consistent and never let him get away with pulling, lagging or sniffing once you have given the heel command. You need to be more determined than he is.

Your dog may show anxiety at this treatment because he may have always pulled on the lead. He cannot understand why things have changed. Do not be concerned by his worried expression; if you give plenty of praise when he is in the right position, he will soon learn which position is preferable and will choose to walk nicely at your side. Persevere. It may take some weeks to eradicate this problem. In time, the word 'No' will be sufficient to make the dog reposition himself and you will not have to check him on the lead. If he fails to respond to the word at any point, you can give the lead a tug.

Some handlers find that passing the lead behind their back to the hand opposite the dog teaches him to walk nicely at heel.

Your heelwork sessions should only last for six minutes. Change direction often. Bribery should accelerate progress. Never finish on a bad note – always stop while he is doing well. If he refuses to cooperate point blank, ask him to do something you know he does well – maybe just the 'Sit'. Then praise him and put him in his quiet place. If you put him away in a bad humour when he has not done well, the memories formed will not be positive.

It is often difficult to stop a dog, and particularly a spaniel, from sniffing as he goes along. Rather than wear themselves out, as long as the dog remains next to them, many people tend to ignore it. A disadvantage is that this may mean that he does not see something you wish he had – the fall of a bird for instance. One thing you can try is to say 'Mark' when he drops his head to sniff, and throw a ball or small dummy ahead of you. As it leaves your hand, say 'Sit'. In this way you are teaching two things – that he should keep his head up and pay attention at all times, and that he should be steady to a throw.

Alternatively you can carry a treat in your hand nearest the dog, and each time he drops his head, say 'Heel' and offer the treat. Sometimes give it and sometimes withhold it. You are trying to teach him that it is preferable to keep his focus on what is around him, not just the scent on the ground. Remember to praise him whenever you see what you want to see.

If a dog has been allowed to pull for a long time, he will have developed a 'hard neck', much as a horse can develop a 'hard mouth'. He no longer feels any discomfort because the nerve endings in the area have become even more insensitive than normal. Carry a rolled-up newspaper, and when he pulls, give him a sharp tap on the side of the muzzle, coupled with your 'No!' A rolled-up newspaper will be a surprise; it will not hurt him but he will not like the sound of it, and it should upset him. After a few repeats, you will probably need do no more than carry the paper and perhaps show it to him occasionally. He will begin to correct himself on the word 'No!'

This method may not sit comfortably with you, and if you are not successful in stopping your dog pulling on the collar and lead, it will be worth investing in a Halti. This is a kind of headcollar for dogs that stops them from lunging forwards. The Halti allows you to control your dog's head, much as a horse is controlled in a halter. Always draw the dog into comfort with a steady pull, not a jerk, when using this training aid. It will not cure the habit of pulling, but will enable you to manage a strong dog when he is on the lead.

Hanging Back or Out to the Side

Sometimes a dog will refuse to come along with you; he just digs his feet in and will not budge. Some will even lie down. Others lean out to one side. None of these ploys is acceptable, and will spoil any outing with your dog.

If persistent pulling out to the side is allowed, it can result in the dog's legs becoming deformed. There is also the hazard of a third party being tripped up by the lead.

The cause is often a reluctance to go towards something the dog fears or dislikes, so you will need to be sympathetic but firm. Use an encouraging voice but do not give in to him. For this problem, use a flat, buckle-on type of collar and a soft strong lead. Be sure the collar is done up snugly.

Try bribery first. Show the dog a treat and keep it just beyond his reach until he comes alongside you. Continue moving forwards. Give the treat to him while you are moving, and be very free with your praise. If he halts or pulls out from you again, say 'No!' and offer the treat again, but when he catches up with you, say 'Heel' but keep the treat from him until he has walked a few paces close to you. As long as the bribe gets him on to his feet, or brings him closer, carry on until you can walk about the length of a tennis court before he has his reward.

If bribery alone does not work, you will need to add correction. It will be like the donkey handler with the carrot and the stick, except you will use the lead instead of a stick, and praise and treats instead of a carrot.

Vigilance is key. If you are quick enough with your correction, it should surprise him into moving into the correct position, and this is when you must praise, repeat 'Heel', and perhaps give him a treat.

Do not accept anything less than the proper position. If you give him leeway, he will take advantage of your leniency. You may have to drag him after you but you should insist – he will eventually cooperate. Moving in a small circle may help to start him off, then continue in your chosen direction. Do the exercise three or four times, then put him in his quiet place for at least two hours. The next day he should be much more compliant.

Poor On Lead but Good Off

People often tell me that their dog pulls on the lead but walks nicely beside them when he is off the lead. This is because on lead, the dog does not have to think about where his handler is; he relies on the tension in the lead to tell him. Off the lead, he must have his handler in his peripheral vision to know his position.

This behaviour shows that the handler is not vigilant or consistent, and dogs will always take advantage of this. Teach your dog to walk on a slack lead. Do *not* say 'Heel' when the dog is out of position: say 'No!' and correct him with a sharp tug. Do not let him get away with going so much as an inch from the correct position.

Good On Lead but Poor Off

Some dogs walk beautifully on the lead, but once let off they begin to sniff, lag or wander. Using titbits can be very useful in keeping a dog's attention during heelwork off lead, but be sparing. Just letting him know that you have treats with you is often enough.

When your dog is walking nicely to heel on lead, reach down, without stopping, and as surreptitiously as possible, unclip the lead from the collar. As you unclip, say 'Heel' and continue walking for five paces. Then say 'Sit' and stop. As you move forwards again, say 'Heel' and just hook your finger in the collar to start the dog walking with you, then let go. After five more paces, stop and tell him to sit. Repeat this several times and then call it a day. Put him in his quiet place.

The reason for only going five paces is that you will maintain control. After that, a dog's mind starts to wander and so will he. As time goes on, you will gradually increase the distance you walk between stops, but be cautious. Always put the lead back on at the first hint of waywardness. This is not a sign that you have failed; you are just ensuring obedience. You can praise for obedience, which will ensure progress. You cannot praise him if he is in the wrong position.

Dancing and Prancing at Heel

Some dogs jump about at heel and make little lunges forward as if they might run in, or they dance with their front feet like a circus horse. This can be distracting to the handler, especially if he is shooting or in a competition.

You need to be very calm, as you are trying to counteract the dog's excitement. Use a flat collar and soft lead. As soon as he begins to prance or lunge, stop walking and pull him back with a steady pull, not a jerk, saying 'Calm down' in a steady voice. Give him a treat if he complies. If he cannot focus on you, apply the muzzle-hold for at least ten seconds, then gently and slowly release. Stop and repeat every time he goes wrong.

Overcoming this behaviour is actually changing your dog's attitude – you are trying to make him conquer his excitement and discipline himself. It may take you some time, but be determined and vigilant. You need to notice every instance of his becoming overwrought and act immediately to calm him.

'Weaving' at Heel

Sometimes a dog that is supposed to be at heel will move from one side to the other behind his handler in the hope of seeing better what is about to happen. You never know where to look for him and he is almost certain to be in the wrong place to be able to mark if a wounded bird falls.

Carry a rolled-up newspaper in the hand opposite the side on which the dog should be. Every time he shows up on the wrong side, give him a quick tap on the nose, saying 'No!' and then call him nicely back to the correct side. If you are consistent, you should soon cure the fault.

Biting or Chewing the Lead

If the lead is in your dog's mouth, you cannot use it effectively. Many a lead is bitten through and this is expensive. A dog can do this so quietly and quickly, you do not realise you are no longer connected to him until you go to move off. If such a dog needs to be tied up, he must be on a chain because he bites through anything else. It is not comfortable to train with a chain lead and at some point a dog may be hit in the face by it, however unintentionally, so set about curing the problem. You must notice the first sign that the dog is about to take hold of the lead and act immediately.

Most puppies will try to take the lead in their mouth when you first put it on. Discourage this by gently removing the lead and offering a treat in exchange. Then keep the pup's attention on you by carrying a biscuit in your closed hand near his face.

If your dog regularly bites the lead, you will need to be firm. Say 'No!' sharply and remove the lead from his mouth. You should not snatch the lead out of the dog's mouth as you could damage his teeth or lips. Put a finger in his mouth behind the lead and press down on his tongue, or if you cannot get your finger in behind the lead, press his lips on either side of his muzzle against his teeth until he opens his mouth and lets go. Straightaway raise the hand holding the lead and lift his head, keeping the lead taut from above for a few seconds. Each time he goes to snatch the lead, say 'No!' firmly but not loudly, and lift his head upwards. Praise him for his cooperation.

Aggressive on Lead but Friendly when Free

When on lead, some dogs seem to feel possessive of their handlers, and more confident of their strength if they are tied up. When they are free, they feel they must rely on themselves alone and are not so brave.

At the first show of this type of aggression, scold the dog and apply the muzzle-hold to make him feel less assertive and to remind him that you are the one in charge. An alternative is to use a Halti. It exerts pressure over the top of the muzzle and so simulates the muzzle-hold. Keep your dog close to you so that he can see that you are cross with him and not with the other dog. If he is at lead's length and hears you scolding, he is sure to think you are backing him up against the other dog, and that the tension in the lead is caused by the other dog! Hopefully the other dog will be on a lead as well and both owners can take their dog away in different directions.

If the other dog is loose and attacks your dog, act as advised in the section on aggression in the previous chapter.

THE SIT

The Sit is the cornerstone of a gundog's training. If your dog will sit and remain sitting whenever and wherever he is asked, he is under control. The command 'Sit' means that the dog should assume the sitting position immediately and remain in it until told to do something else.

Refusing to Sit on the First Command

When a dog refuses to sit on the first command it is usually because the handler has repeated the sit command more than once in the past without physically putting the dog into the correct position. The dog hears 'Sit, sit, sit' while he is standing and therefore thinks that the word means he can stand. It does not seem to matter to him that the handler's tone is becoming increasingly irritated: it is still the same word. When you give a command and you do not see what you expect – and this includes the other commands too – you must say 'No!' meaningfully, with a correction on the collar. Repeat the command and put the dog into the correct position, physically, and then praise him. This is obviously at close quarters.

If the dog refuses to stop on the whistle at a distance and keeps moving, you must go out to him and insist that he sits. He must sit on the precise spot where he was when he first heard the whistle or voice command, so you need to note that spot and place him there. You then return to your original position, saying 'Sit' several times on your way and blowing the stop whistle every few seconds. Face your dog and praise him, blow the stop whistle once more and then either give him a direction signal to find a dummy, release him, or return to him and congratulate him.

You have to be determined and insist that he comes to a dead halt when you blow the stop whistle, every time. If you are inconsistent, the dog will use poor performance to gain your attention, making you repeat yourself, making you go out to position him. *He will train you* to do whatever goes with his refusing to obey you. And believe me, dogs know how to be consistent in training us!

It will help enormously if your dog sees the point of stopping. Therefore, the instant he sits or stops, make it worth his while by giving him a titbit, or fish out a dummy or a ball to waggle at him. The idea is that you are giving the dog something to look at, a reward for stopping and looking at you. Anyone can teach a dog to sit as a pure discipline at any distance, but we need the dog to stop *and look at us.* When he is steady enough, you can throw the dummy or ball out to one side, insisting that he remains sitting, then after a couple of seconds, say 'Sit' or blow the stop whistle – which means 'Look at me' – then give him the hand signal and command to go and fetch.

If he is not steady, he should wear a flat collar. Stop him on the whistle at about twenty paces from you and produce a small dummy from your pocket and show it to him. Go up to him and note the exact spot where he is. Restrain him with the collar and throw the dummy out to his side. Blow the stop whistle again and, keeping your eye on the dog, walk back to your starting point.

If he moves, you must make every attempt to stop him, using the word 'No!' If he manages to evade you and collect the retrieve, say nothing, just accept the article and walk him back to where he should be sitting. Do not on any account give the sit or recall command when he runs in. If you do and he obeys, you have to praise him. You will not have dealt with the problem of unsteadiness at all. Put him back in his original spot, blow the stop whistle again, reinforcing with the word 'Sit' and your hand raised in the 'Sit' signal. Place the dummy back where it was the first time. Placing it is less likely to excite the dog than throwing it. Retreat carefully and slowly, only going half as far as before. Once there, blow the stop whistle one more time, and then give an arm signal to send him to retrieve.

Rising Immediately when Praised or Restraint is Removed

If your dog moves the moment you say 'Good dog' or take the lead off or let go of his collar, put two leads on him. When you take off the first one he may move, believing he is free, in which case you scold him and check him with the second lead. Replace the first lead, walk him several paces with you and then put him in the sit. Praise him, then repeat the process of taking off the first lead. You may have to repeat this exercise several times, but eventually he should grasp the idea.

When you can take off one lead and he remains sitting, you should be able to replace the first lead, walk him a little way, give the command to sit, praise him and remind him to sit while you remove both leads. Repeat this until you consistently have success three or four times in a row. Put him in his quiet place. Leave him there for at least an hour. Eventually he should realise that he must not move until he hears the release command.

This two-lead method sometimes also works well with a dog that runs in. However, you must be braced for any sudden lunges!

Refusing to Remain Sitting when Handler Moves Away

The most common reason why a dog refuses to remain sitting when the handler moves away is that the handler uses two commands, most often 'Sit' and 'Stay'. These two words mean exactly the same to a human being but a dog thinks he is being offered a choice, and he will almost always choose to do neither. Just say 'Sit' – it means he should sit until he is told to do something else: it means sit until he starves to death! There is no confusion, no inconsistency.

Another reason a dog will move when his handler leaves him is because he is anxious about being left. Build his confidence very gradually by holding the lead so that you can restrain him while you step only one pace away. In fact, you just rock away on to one foot, then back to your dog's side, repeating 'Sit' while you do so and praising him quietly. This is to make the dog understand that he is not being abandoned. Do this several times and then go two steps, but return without delay. If the dog still moves, tie him to a fence post and start with just one step away. Return after a second and

When teaching a dog to remain seated, we need to give him confidence that we are not leaving him forever; we would like him to remain on the spot while we go away and keep still until we return. As with all training, this needs to be done in small stages. Stand close to the dog facing him. Give the command 'Sit', and raise one hand in the signal while holding the end of the lead in the other hand. Keep one foot absolutely still and step back on the other; you just rock away and then bring the moving foot back next to the stationary one. It doesn't seem much but it is a little acorn from which the mighty oak will grow.

Some dogs can be very anxious about the handler moving away and just cannot remain on the spot. A very good shortcut to eliminate this is to tie the dog to a firm gate or fence and then practise the rocking away as in the previous photograph. The dog should be wearing a flat collar that does not tighten on his neck. It should be done up snugly so that he cannot slip out of it. A very anxious dog may be quite upset by this method at first and struggle to free himself, but usually he will quickly realise what you want, especially if you reward him with titbits when he is calm. His confidence will soon build to the level where you can go many yards and be away for some minutes.

reward him with a treat if he has remained still. Next, move two steps and return straightaway and reward. You can see how to build on this, but go slowly so that you make steady progress.

Always put him back in the exact place you originally left him. You should note the spot – sit him next to a weed or a patch of bare earth or a clump of daisies.

Presently, when you see that the dog has grasped what you want, you can begin to teach him to remain still off lead by going back to the beginning and taking baby steps. If you are careful and thorough, he will learn to remain in place indefinitely.

UNSTEADINESS

A steady dog is one that has been conditioned through training to resist any temptation to move from heel or the sit without permission, or to chase in any situation. Steadiness applies to retrievers when they are at heel, sitting or out hunting. It applies to spaniels when they are quartering or retrieving. It also applies to the pointing and setting breeds in that they must resist any temptation to chase, especially when the game they have been 'holding' flushes. If two or more dogs are questing for game and one dog comes on point, the others should 'back' him – that is, they should copy the first dog. This is also called 'honouring the point', and the backing dogs must remain as steady as the first dog.

Some pointers are too staunch on point – it is as if they are in a trance. When encouraged to 'Road in', they are reluctant to move and will do so only slowly, needing

much encouragement. Clicking your fingers in front of the dog's face may help to break the spell. Another type of dog is too keen and should be restrained with the lead so that he walks at your pace. You should be ready to give the command for the dog to sit as soon as game begins to flush.

If your retrieving dog has run in on many occasions, he has fulfilled his instincts and repetition has caused an enduring habit. It is doubtful that you will ever make him reliably steady. If you truly wish to try and overcome the problem, you must go back to the beginning, changing your command and teaching the dog afresh. Steadiness is fully covered in my first book, *In the Bag!*.

In time you may succeed in training your dog to be steady to the fall of dead game. However, a runner will eventually drop and he will not be able to resist temptation.

If you are a Gun, you may have success in stopping him running in if you sacrifice your shooting for several outings and concentrate solely on your dog. That said, when you feel confident enough to shoot over him, you will be changing the whole picture, and sadly, he will almost certainly revert.

If picking up, you must tell your colleagues that you will not be able to participate properly. You must only have the unsteady dog with you, and must give him your complete attention. Watch for the smallest hint that he is about to run in, and correct him sincerely. But even when you feel that he is cooperating with you, you will probably find that when you add another dog to the mix, the dog you have spent so much time on will think everything has changed and he will start running in again.

A dog that must be kept on lead may jump about or lunge forwards to free himself. This is totally unacceptable as it can result in serious injury to the handler or others in the vicinity.

You must not take chances with such a dog when shooting is in progress. Put a check chain and a soft but strong lead on him, and be ready to brace yourself and correct him meaningfully. If you are shooting or are not strong enough to hold him, tie him to something solid, such as the towbar of a vehicle or a straining post. You will probably have to use a chain – he will chew through a leather or fabric lead in seconds. The corkscrew type of stake used

Insisting on Obedience?

A farmer was driving his horse and cart to market with his dog sitting beside him. All of a sudden a hare jumped up in front of the horse. The dog jumped down from his seat and took off in hot pursuit. The farmer shouted at the dog to stop but it was in vain. 'Get on, you brute,' he yelled. 'You will obey!'

to tether a dog at the peg will not do – it is not unusual to see one of these bouncing along behind an errant dog! Obviously, tying the dog up is not a cure – it is merely management. It does not lend itself to the enjoyment of your day, and it is probably best to leave the dog at home.

The use of a Halti should enable you to restrain a dog without having to secure him to something immovable. Do not tie up your dog when he is in a Halti – he will be able to chew through it in a trice and free himself. Even a Halti may not be the answer – some dogs are very clever and learn to face their handler and pull strongly backwards! This dog should also be left at home.

ANTICIPATION

There are many examples of anticipation. In early training of the recall you may have taught the dog to sit while you walk away. At a certain distance, you turn and call him to you. Quite soon the dog sees you begin to turn, and he is on his way to you. He is anticipating that you are about to call him. The remedy is to say 'Sit' as you are about to turn, and to hold your hand up in the 'sit' signal. Keep him sitting for several seconds before you call. Alternatively, walk further away or back towards him before you call. Keep him guessing.

Another example is when you have stopped the dog on the whistle at a distance in order to redirect him. He sees you raise your arm, but before you have completed the signal, he has set off in the direction he hopes is right. Whether it is right or wrong, you should stop him again or, best policy, take him back to his original spot and make him remain in place until he has seen the whole of your signal. *See* Chapter 9, the section 'Dog Refuses to Take Direction Signals Correctly'.

Sometimes when a dog is really excited about imminent 'release' or freedom – perhaps you have him at heel but you are close to the gateway where you usually let him have free time – he will suddenly dart forwards unbidden. In effect, this is running in. You must be ready for such anticipation and begin reminding him to remain with you by saying 'Heel' every few paces until you suddenly surprise him by saying 'Run on'. Make sure you ring the changes often so that he becomes more focused on you and forgets about anticipating.

THE RECALL

The recall command is equally as important as 'Sit'. A dog that will turn on its heel at the sound of the recall command or whistle signal is under control and will not cause problems on a shoot or anywhere else.

Ignoring the Recall Command or Whistle Signal

This problem is covered in Chapter 7, 'Dog Gone!'.

Dashing Past Handler or Dancing around Just out of Reach

A dog usually starts this behaviour because he does not understand what you want.

Put the flat collar on the dog and do it up snugly. Tie a length of cord or baler twine to the collar. It should be about a metre long so that you can catch hold of it or step on it when the dog is avoiding you. When you have the cord in your hand, reel him in, praising him. Give him a treat as soon as he is close enough, and repeat the word 'Come' several times while you keep him near you.

He may keep too far from you to catch hold of the cord, and he may start barking. Barking usually indicates that the dog is confused. He may look defiant, but that is not an emotion that dogs show, and it is a look that means he does not understand. He may try to turn things into a game. If you persist in speaking to this type of dog, or even looking at him, he will realise that he is receiving attention. Therefore, as long as you are in a safe place, immediately he begins barking, turn and walk or run away and go somewhere he cannot join you. Leave him for at least ten minutes. That will give *you* time to calm down if you need it, and he will realise that you are not giving him the attention he would like.

When you return, take a treat or toy with you to show him that things have changed. Offer the toy or titbit, and hopefully he will let you take hold of his collar. Do about five minutes heelwork, on lead, offering treats frequently so he develops a good association with being near you. Then shut him in his quiet place for at least an hour.

For at least a week after this, put the lead on every time you take him out. Make each outing pleasant in every possible way so he thinks that you are good to be with, and he should begin to want to cooperate with you generally. Do not abandon the lead too soon. It is better to keep him on lead for too long than not long enough.

When you begin trying him off lead, have him in a small enclosure with the short cord trailing. Be free with your praise and treats. Practise in different enclosures each day for two weeks. He will eventually understand that it is preferable to come. You can build on success but not on failure.

CHAPTER **9** Handling Troubles

Having covered problems with the three foundation commands of 'Heel', 'Sit' and 'Come' we move on to the difficulties that can crop up with more advanced gundog training.

REFUSING TO STOP ON THE WHISTLE

One of the most common problems I see in gundogs is refusing to stop at a distance. If you have no brakes, you have no steering.

Although sheepdogs can be taught to change direction while on the move, our gundog acts better if he is stopped before being redirected. The sheepdog needs to keep his eye on the sheep – or whatever he is herding – and he is responding as much to their movement as he is to the shepherd. He and the shepherd work closely as a team, and his instinct is to be in the right place to turn the sheep. The shepherd is there to help the dog move the sheep to the required place. Incidentally, the sheepdog must drop to the stop whistle or command immediately, again to ensure that the sheep do not go in the wrong direction. Most sheepdogs are more reliable at this than many of our gundogs.

While the gundog is also working with his handler, he is not relying on sight to the same degree as the sheepdog. He is relying almost entirely on his nose. The handler is endeavouring to place him in a position where he will be able to find the scent of the retrieve. This might well be counter to the dog's instincts. His instinct is to try to find scent using the wind, and this could take him well away from the correct area. We need to be able to stop the dog and have his eye on us so that he can be directed by signals and sometimes verbal commands to set off in a new direction.

The advantage of having a dog you can redirect is enormous – it saves time and energy, yours and the dog's, and you should not just shrug your shoulders and give up. Having a dog that will stop and take directions means he

will collect game without delay – this is especially important when it comes to runners.

With a young dog, you generally have three chances. If you stop him and redirect him three times and he does not find the retrieve, he will usually give up on you and ignore the whistle the next time you blow it. For this reason, you must be certain of the whereabouts of the retrieve so that you will be telling the truth when you direct the dog. He needs to develop confidence and trust in your apparent gift for knowing the exact location of the prize. Second, it is vital that he understands your signals correctly. If these two things are right, your dog will probably find within the three chances. Once you have helped him to find the retrieve a few times, he will become more reliable on the stop whistle, and eventually he will stop every time he hears it. Making it preferable to him to stop is the key. He needs to understand that you can help him if he stops and looks at you.

A common difficulty is caused when the handler blows the whistle louder or longer for emphasis. More is *not* better, it is just different. If the whistle does not sound the way the dog is used to hearing it, he will not recognise it and will probably disobey.

See the section 'Refusing to Sit on the First Command', in Chapter 8.

REFUSING TO LOOK AT THE HANDLER ON STOPPING

If your dog will stop when at a distance from you but will not look at you, it is because he does not understand why you have stopped him. He is just stopping out of pure discipline. The remedy is very similar to that discussed in the last section. The dog needs you to show him something worthwhile. If you do not address this situation, he will not only refuse to look at you, but will cease to stop because he sees no gain in it for him. You then have a dual problem.

You must insist that he always stops completely. Nothing more happens until he does. I have found that when a dog will not stop to the whistle or voice command, he will often stop if you make the 'Brrrrrr!' sound that is used to catch a dog's attention when a dummy is thrown. When he has stopped and he looks at you, produce a dummy, blow your stop whistle again – it means 'look at me' – and throw the dummy out to his side, reminding him to remain still. Blow again and when he is looking at you, give a clear signal and command for him to retrieve. Make sure he sees the whole signal.

Gradually, the distance at which you expect the dog to stop and take directions should be increased. He may fail to stop when he is further from you, but using the 'Brrrrr!' sound usually helps. When he does stop, he may be too far away for you to throw the dummy effectively, which rewards him for looking at you. A tennis-ball thrower or a dummy launcher may come in handy in this situation, always assuming that your dog is steady to flying objects. Alternatively, you can walk out until you are close enough to place a dummy where you want it and then return to your old position, blow the stop whistle and give your signal.

If the ball or dummy you are throwing to gain his interest lands at an angle less or more than a right angle from you, you should move until your hand signal points that important parallel line. *See* the section 'Commands and Signals for All Dogs' in Chapter 4.

REFUSING TO TAKE DIRECTION SIGNALS CORRECTLY

Once a dog has learned the meanings of the hand signals, he will seldom deliberately go the wrong way unless there are distractions.

Sometimes a dog goes the wrong way when you have signalled him because he has 'found you out'. At some point in the past you may have directed him one way, but because he has winded a retrieve in another direction, he has turned that way and picked it. This will make him doubt you, and he will be disinclined to go the way you indicate for ever after. While you are teaching or reteaching signals, make sure that he cannot pick up scent in a direction other than the one in which you wish him to go. Arrange it so that the wind is helping him.

If your dog often goes the wrong way, you must examine the way you give your signals. Quite commonly, a handler will stop the dog successfully on the whistle at a distance, then raise his hand in front of him, move it slightly across his body to one side, and then throw it out to the side he intended. For example, the dog needs to move to his left in order to find the retrieve: the handler stops him, brings his right hand up in front of his chest, moves it slightly to his left and then throws it out to his right. The dog, being quick, sees the slight movement of the handler's hand to the left and takes off in that direction without seeing the intended signal. *See* the section 'Commands Associated with Retrieving' in Chapter 4.

If you are guilty of this you must change. *Before* you blow the stop whistle, you should raise your signalling arm from your side, elbow straight, until it is level with your shoulder, pointing out to the side. Blow the stop whistle, and when the dog looks at you, give your verbal command – 'right' or 'left' – and give a small waggle of the hand. This should start the dog moving in the correct direction.

To accentuate what you want, you can move your foot sideways in the appropriate direction and lean your body too. Always keep your eye on the dog; do not look at your hand or the retrieve. If the dog does not seem to understand, go closer to him and try again.

The command 'Get on', meaning 'Go straight away from me', is coupled with an upward flick of your hand as high as you can reach. Other handlers use a high pushing motion. Both are fine as long as they are higher than your head so there is no confusion with the 'Sit' signal. The hand signal for 'Sit' should never be higher than your forehead: your palm faces the dog and should be level with your face so that to the dog, at a distance, your face and your hand appear as two oval blobs, side by side.

Another reason why a dog may not act on a signal is that he has never seen it. When we are teaching a dog to move left, right or straight ahead on hand signals, we often use dummies he has seen us throw or place. We sit the dog and put out a dummy and then walk a certain distance from the dog. We face him and raise an arm to send him, and like a bullet from a gun, he has gone. He did not see the whole signal so he was not able to learn it.

For a sideways retrieve, place or throw the dummy about 10 metres from the dog, and then position yourself fifteen or twenty paces from the dog at 90 degrees to the dog from the dummy. Usually the dog will be looking steadfastly towards the dummy. Raise the arm you intend to signal with to shoulder height, and blow the

Wrong. The handler wishes the dog to go to the right (his right) but he has raised his right arm with the elbow bent so that his hand is pointing towards his left.

Wrong. The dog has seen the movement of the hand to the handler's left and sets off in what she believes is the required direction.

Correct. The correct way to raise your arm for the signal is up from your side with your elbow kept straight. The arm should be raised at the same moment that you blow the stop whistle so that when the dog looks at you, you are ready to give the signal.

Correct. The handler is adding emphasis to his signal by leaning his body in the direction required. Note that his left arm is kept close and still so as not to create any confusion on the dog's part. The same procedure applies when asking the dog to travel to the handler's left, but of course using the opposite arm and body signalling.

stop whistle to gain his attention. The toot means, 'Look at me, I'm going to show you something worth your while.' The 'something' is your hand signal. Very often your dog is so focused on the dummy that he refuses to look at you, but you must insist that he does. As soon as he looks at you, waggle your hand to send him and say 'right' or 'left' as appropriate. This way, he sees the point of looking at you. Be sure to make the dog wait until you give the whole signal and your command. If he does not wait, he will not see the signal and he will not learn it. If he sees the whole movement, he will learn the meaning.

If you are teaching the dog to go further away, you will be using the 'Get on' command and the high flick of your hand. Once he is positioned and the dummy is placed beyond him, move fifteen to twenty paces from him and make sure that he is in a straight line from you to the dummy. Before you blow the stop whistle, raise your arm above your head. Again, he may be staring at the dummy and you may have to use the whistle and much verbal encouragement before he will look at you. As soon as he does, give an upward flick of your hand and your verbal command to encourage him to move off to retrieve.

In the case of either the sideways or 'Get on' signals, insist that he does not anticipate and set off before he has seen *the entire signal. See* Chapter 4, 'Commands Associated with Retrieving' section.

If your dog happens to look at you when you blow the stop whistle and before you have raised your arm, you must repeat your sit command over and over as you slowly raise the arm. Do not allow him to move until you are ready to give the very last part of the signal and your word of command.

You should not allow the dog to make off in the wrong direction: he will soon be floundering about and you will be stopping him over and over to no avail. Not surprisingly, you will probably become cross and frustrated, which is always counter-productive. He may find the retrieve by chance, but that just will not do: he must find it on your terms. At the first deviation, blow your stop whistle and go out to him and apply the muzzle-hold for a few seconds, speaking to him quietly and reassuringly. Then take him towards the retrieve until he perceives it by sight or scent. Say 'Heel' to him, and walk him back to the last spot he was sitting. Say 'Sit' to him, and blow the whistle and walk back to your starting place. Turn towards him and wait for a few seconds so he is really settled, then blow the stop whistle and give the appropriate signal and

verbal command. The more measured you are in this, the better your chance of conveying what you mean.

In the early stages, most young dogs will not move off when sitting away from you, even with considerable encouragement. The reason for this is that they think it is wrong to leave the sitting position unless they are beside you. After all, up to now, your dog has always been sent from next to you. Many dogs, when they do move, come towards you and then move off to make the retrieve. They do this in an attempt to put themselves in what they believe is the correct position – by your side – from which to go for a retrieve. They deviate to run in a horseshoe pattern eventually reaching the dummy, collecting it and returning to you. Do not worry about this – your dog will soon realise that the shortest distance between two points is a straight line.

It is a puzzle to me that some handlers do not like using the commands 'Right' and 'Left'. Perhaps they feel they cannot be sure they are saying the correct word. Many of us confuse our left and right, but I have found that using these commands has made me learn them properly. Perhaps those opposed to using these commands think that using these words is too much like circus tricks – but a Martian might think that all our training was circus tricks – and so what? However, many of these critical handlers do like the idea of using directional commands, and teach their dog 'Away' or 'Come by' instead. These are the words shepherds use. Some of us would have as much trouble remembering which meant which direction as we do with right and left!

Of course, you could teach your dog to change direction on whistle signals. After all, teaching a dog to turn and come to you is a case in point. Similarly, it is common practice to teach a spaniel or other questing dog to change direction on the whistle when hunting.

It is quite a refinement if your dog will obey these directional words or whistle signals on a very cold day as you can keep your hands in your pockets!

REFUSING TO LOOK WHERE THE HANDLER IS INDICATING

When you are about to cast out your dog on an unseen retrieve, you should make absolutely certain that he is looking in the direction you are pointing. His muzzle should be parallel to your hand and he should have complete focus on the direction you wish him to take. This is called 'locking on'. *See* Chapter 11, 'Lack of Confidence in Going Out on Unseen Retrieves'.

Refusing to 'lock on' often occurs on a shoot day when excitement levels are high and the dog finds it difficult to focus. His blood is up and he is distracted. If you are a Gun, time is usually not on your side, but if you can, take the dog towards the retrieve you wish him to collect, and with luck you will be able to place him in a downwind position so that he can catch scent of the bird. You may then be able to achieve his cooperation: he will look where you indicate, you send him, and he will succeed. It may take several repetitions but eventually he will believe that you can help him.

If you do not have time to do this, make sure a picker-up knows about the bird so that it will be picked. If you are a picker-up, you can use the situation to teach your dog that you know a thing or two.

Do not allow your dog to set off when he has not 'locked on'. He will go the way he decides and you will end up stopping and redirecting him, probably several times, or he will ignore you and gain his prize. Thereafter it will be an uphill struggle for you to disabuse him of his belief that he is right and you are wrong.

At home, go back to basics and teach him to ignore the seen retrieve and to go where you indicate. Eventually he will realise that whichever way you point him, he will gain his reward.

THE DISTANCE BARRIER

It is very common for a young dog that usually stops well on the whistle, to begin refusing to do so when he reaches a certain distance from his handler. Or if he does stop, he fails to take hand signals correctly. I call this 'the distance barrier' because it is as if the dog comes to an invisible wall that he can go through, but beyond which he is all at sea regarding following directions. Do not despair: it is just a matter of gradually building his confidence to work with you outside a certain range.

Dogs need to work in lots of different places before they realise that the same rules apply wherever they are, and this includes working at increasing distances. It includes sending a dog out of sight to work; this might be into a wood or over the brow of a hill. Helping your dog to learn to work outside what is effectively his comfort zone may involve you in walking considerable distances, many times, to show him that he will be sure to find the prize if he follows your instructions.

Memory retrieves will be your chief way of teaching him. Increase the distances very gradually, always ensuring that he finds the retrieve with a minimum of delay. Try to make conditions in his favour as much as you can. For example, work him across the wind so that he will find scent as he passes below the retrieve. Each time he succeeds gives him more confidence to cooperate with you.

Having someone to help you is a very effective way of extending your dog's range. Give your helper a supply of dummies and ask him to stand in plain view. Position your dog about twenty paces short of your assistant. Make a note of this spot as you will need to put him there again. You should then walk away in the opposite direction until you are at the crucial limit, face your dog and blow the stop whistle. After a moment, the helper should make the 'Brrrrrr!' noise, or he can say 'Mark', and slap the dummy so that the dog looks towards him. As he looks, the helper should throw the dummy further away, outside the dog's distance barrier.

You may need to move sideways so that the dog is in a straight line to the retrieve. Blow the stop whistle, and when the dog looks at you, but not before, give the 'Get on' signal and command. Because the dog has just seen the dummy, he will be keen to go before he has seen the entire signal so you must be careful that he waits until he has seen it. He will almost certainly go without hesitation and make the retrieve. Repeat this sequence three or four times, using a different dummy each time. Every time the dog succeeds helps to set the lesson in his mind.

If the dog does not go straight to fetch the dummy, looks confused or goes off at a tangent, go out to him and settle him on his spot again. Only go back half the distance to your starting point and blow the stop whistle. Ask your assistant to call out and throw another dummy. Now there are two possible retrieves, which gives your dog a better chance of finding quickly. Making sure the dog is in a direct line to the fall of the last dummy, blow your 'Sit' signal again and give the 'Get on' signal and command.

It may be that the dog still does not see the point and you will have to replace him on his spot, another dummy will need to be thrown, and now there will be three dummies out. Reduce the distance that you stand from him. Eventually the dog will go and pick one. He may find another and swap – don't worry, it will all come right in the end.

By positioning yourself closer to the dog, thereby putting him inside his comfort zone, he will be more likely to carry out the 'Get on' command, but having an assistant means that you can quite quickly recommence extending the range. Practise this exercise in several different places and on three or four consecutive days. Gradually introduce variations, such as sending him through gateways, across water, into cover or woodland or over the brow of a hill.

When you are training on your own, a long and fairly straight footpath will be very useful in overcoming the distance barrier. Place your dog in the 'Sit' on the path and let him see you throw or place a dummy about twenty paces further along. Walk away in the opposite direction, leaving your dog between you and the retrieve. Go to your dog's critical distance and face him. Blow your stop whistle and give the 'Get on' signal. The dog will almost certainly go and retrieve.

Repeat the procedure a few times, each time increasing the distance you are from the dog and the dummy is from the dog. As he becomes more confident, start to place the dummy less conspicuously. If he falters at any stage, you should revert to placing the dummy so that it shows up clearly to him. Eventually he will go without hesitation and as far as you ask.

Until now, your dog has been stationary when you have sent him on from his limit to the retrieve. Now you need to teach him to act for you when he is on the move.

On your path, throw or place a dummy just behind you for him to see. Walk on with him for twenty paces and sit him down. Leave him there and go to the limit of his comfort zone. Call him towards you, and although he may be thinking about the dummy, insist that he starts to come towards you. When he has come a few metres, blow your stop whistle and raise your hand in the 'Sit' signal. Praise him for stopping, and then without any hurry and making sure that he sees the whole signal, raise your hand high, give the flick, and say 'Get on'. He should be happy to go and collect the retrieve. Use this exercise sparingly, because if you do it too often, the dog will become 'sticky': he will anticipate that you are going to stop him and will slow down and perhaps stop without being asked. Make sure to ring the changes in all aspects of training so that the dog is kept guessing.

In the next phase, a helper will enable you to make the best progress. Position him with a selection of dummies at a point where he can throw dummies in plain view to land in rough grass. Take your dog approximately forty paces away from your helper. Give your release command and encourage the dog to run about. When he is a few metres from you, blow your stop whistle, and when he is sitting, ask your helper to make the 'Brrrrrr!' noise: when the dog looks at him, he should throw a dummy out to his side. You must then move away from your dog until you have increased the distance between you to his critical point. Keep him in a line between you and the retrieve. Blow your stop whistle and raise your sending arm high. When the dog looks at you, give the flick and the 'Get on' command.

You can also use this method to practise the right and left directional signals. When the dummy has been thrown, you move yourself until you are at right angles through the dog to the fall. You can increase the radius within which he acts well by gradually moving further from your helper and allowing the dog to run about for longer before you stop him.

Of course, you can also send him for a dummy he has seen thrown and stop him on the way. You then send him on to it, but you must only do this once in a while so as to prevent the dog from anticipating. You want him to go out with panache and drive.

Occasionally, a dog that you believe has overcome the 'distance barrier' will begin to show the old signs when he is on new ground. Do not despair, just go out to where he checks and send him on from there. As he begins to carry on in the right direction, you can slowly retire to your original position. The more you practise in different places, the more confident he will become.

See Chapter 11, the section 'Lack of Confidence in Going Out for Unseen Retrieves'. *See also* 'Refusing to Stop on the Whistle' at the beginning of this chapter.

REFUSING TO FACE THE WIND

Most dogs dislike working directly into the wind. They know instinctively, or learn early on, that scent fans out as it drifts downwind, and this means they are likely to perceive more molecules when working across the wind. We need to build the dog's confidence so he will face the wind and reach the correct area as quickly as possible. If he keeps tacking right and left it will obviously take more time and may mean the loss of a wounded bird. It may also mean that he could stray into an area of unshot game, and that could lead to trouble.

Begin by working him straight into a gentle breeze, a short distance from the retrieve. Finding it quickly will encourage him. Gradually increase the distances, always ensuring he succeeds with the minimum of delay.

Working Against the Elements

One of the best retrieves I ever saw was made by Allie Hogsbjerg's yellow Labrador, Subridge Rocket, at an Open field trial at Windsor. The wind and rain were driving straight towards us and the retrieves were some 200 metres ahead. Once the dogs had gone 100 metres, it was almost impossible to see them. The light was poor and dogs had difficulty seeing their handlers and had to respond to whistle and voice. Subridge Rocket showed that he had been well trained and had confidence in his handler. He went the distance with a minimum of assistance and picked his bird. This proved to be a three-dog eye-wipe and he subsequently won the trial.

Move on to training him in higher winds and all kinds of weather.

Many dogs 'fall off the wind' instead of maintaining a direct course, and some handlers make allowance for this by casting them out higher on the wind. This has its merits, but if for some reason the dog stays on course he will have to be redirected when closer to the retrieve in order to place him in a downwind position.

Even if you cast him directly towards the retrieve and he keeps straight, he may just miss scenting the retrieve – perhaps he was breathing out when he should have been breathing in – but if you are sure of the fall, call him back towards you a little and when you are sure he is downwind of the fall, cast him out again. With luck he will catch its scent on the next pass.

PROBLEMS WITH JUMPING

Some handlers use the word 'Over' when their dog comes to an obstacle and they want him to get through or over it. It could a hedge, fence or bank. They use 'Over' when they want the dog to go out of water on the far side and up the bank. It means, 'Negotiate that barrier.' Others use 'Get on' or 'Back' to mean, 'Continue away from me regardless of what is in the way.' Others say 'Over' as they send their dog out, meaning, 'Look for an obstacle and get through or over it.' Each method has its merits.

I belong to the first group. I feel that you should be consistent in the way you cast the dog from your side, and then when the barrier or obstacle is in the dog's sight, that is the time to tell him he needs to deal with it. It seems to me that it encourages him if you give him a specific command at the right moment. After all, you will have taught him your word for jumping in a certain way at the beginning, and it will be unlike your method of casting him. When you are teaching him to jump, the picture the dog has of you indicating the obstacle will probably be you pointing closely at it, even patting it, to encourage him to jump over it. If it is made easy, most dogs quickly learn to love jumping and then it is not a problem to have them jumping more and more difficult obstacles at increasing distances.

If you have a dog that is afraid of jumping or going through a hedge, go back to the beginner stage and make it easy. Try him over a log on the ground or through a very thin hedge with no spikey bits. Use treats freely and lots of praise, but do not ask him to retrieve over any obstacle until you see he is confident and enjoying

When a dog is learning to jump, it will give him confidence if he is asked to collect small, light articles.

This picture shows a dog 'banking' the jump – in other words, half-landing with his hind feet on the top and pushing off. This is fine on a wall or wooden bar, but not good when jumping wire. When your dog is very young and you are asking him to jump small obstacles, try to teach him to jump clear by being very pleased when he does, but grumble a bit when he banks the jump. If he makes a habit of jumping clear, he should keep out of trouble. This is especially valuable if he is out of sight of you.

himself. This may not happen on the first day, and the first time you ask him to retrieve from the other side, be sure to use a tennis ball or a very small light dummy so he is not encumbered by weight or shape.

Jumping wire fencing is best avoided but sometimes there is no alternative. It is a valuable accomplishment if your dog can clear a wire fence because there will come a time when he has gone out of sight to hunt and comes to a fence. If he is in hot pursuit of game he will attempt to jump it, and if he has not been taught properly, he can come to real harm.

Begin with a very low fence and encourage him to take a good run at it so that he clears it. If he 'banks' it – puts his hind feet on the top to push off from it – he can easily injure himself or be caught in the wire. Make it fun by praising enthusiastically and using treats. As you gradually ask him to tackle higher wire, he may balk. It will help if you hang a sheet or blanket over the wire to make it look solid. You should still try to encourage him to jump cleanly.

Avoid barbed wire if you can, but if there is no other way, take your coat off and lay it over the wire so it cannot hurt the dog as he goes over. Having said that, I have known dogs that avoid the coat somehow and jump the

This dog has learnt that I will praise him for jumping clear.

When negotiating a wire fence, a dog will sometimes be caught up by putting a foot through on the take-off side and ending up with his body hanging on the far side. This can be a very serious situation. Placing a coat over a wire fence will prevent this, but try to place it so there is no chance of the dog avoiding the coat and still jumping the wire. Here we have a stile with an upright and another person to the dog's left, and the handler standing pressing the fence down on the dog's right. This encourages the dog to jump the coat. Note that the handler's hands are close to her body so that if the dog banks the jump, she will not rake her mistress's hands with her claws. Note also that the dog on the near side is sitting politely and not interfering.

In this instance, the dog on our side of the fence has not been told to sit still and he is interfering with the jumping dog and the people helping.

Holding up the bottom strand of wire is another way of helping a dog to negotiate a fence.

wire before you can stop them! Make sure other dogs keep clear so they don't put off the jumper or interfere with him.

An important part of a gundog's education is learning to stop on the whistle and take a hand signal to turn to one side and jump an obstacle to his right or left. This will often take him into cover or woodland, and he must learn to continue into it in order to find the retrieve. You should practise this first at very close quarters with seen retrieves, and gradually build up the dog's courage to go out of sight to hunt.

The same applies to going over a stream and out of sight to hunt.

REFUSING TO RETURN OVER OBSTACLES

This is akin to training a dog to return over water the way he went. Choose a low jump and place the dog on the other side of it from you. You should stand right against your side of the jump. Using small treats, encourage the dog to come to you over the obstacle. Your word should be 'Over'. When he is on your side, throw another treat a short distance over the jump and say 'Over', and when he has picked it up, call him and say 'Over' again. Do this four or five times, using a small treat every time and lots of praise. You should use an enthusiastic tone, and hopefully the dog will soon see it as great fun.

Next, use a tennis ball or small dummy, but be sure to throw it so it lands only a short distance the far side of the jump. As before, you should be very close to your side of the jump. Send your dog and then step right up to the obstacle and encourage him to return over it. Be sincere with your praise and you should soon find that he is keen to do it the way you would like.

REFUSING TO ENTER WATER OR SWIM

Jumping into water and swimming is definitely a summer job. You want the experience to be pleasant for your dog and not bitterly cold for you! Go to a shallow pond or stream with other friendly dogs that enjoy water, and encourage them all to play in the water together. Your dog may still refuse to go in, but he should feel envious watching the others having fun. If he follows them, well and good, but whether he goes in or not, make sure you

Taking a puppy with other dogs that enjoy water will encourage him to enjoy it too.

shut him in his quiet place for at least an hour after-wards. He will reflect on the outing, and if he was reluc-tant the first time, he may be happy to join in next time.

If he will not follow the other dogs, call them up and put them away. Take your problem dog on his own to shallow water. You should be wearing wellington boots or, better still, waders and you should have his favourite treats in your pocket. Have a snug-fitting flat collar on him, and a lead about a metre long. Have him at heel and wade into the water, speaking kindly to him and saying 'Get in' as you go. He may resist strenuously, but hold the collar firmly and speak softly, and draw him in till he is close to you. Give him lots of soothing praise. He

should only be in the water up to his hocks. Offer him a treat – he will probably refuse it but it is still a nice idea. If he does take it, you are reinforcing that entering water is a nice experience. After perhaps a minute, lead him out again – he may lunge ahead towards dry land but try to keep him close to you.

Throwing a few biscuits on to the water sometimes tempts a dog to go in for them, but the water should be very shallow at first. If this trick works, you can gradu-ally increase the distance he will go for the biscuits, and eventually the depth too.

You may have to repeat this day after day for sev-eral days before he goes in happily. Always keep your temper and be pleasant. It is so tempting just to throw a dog in, but that is unlikely to work – probably you will just frighten him. You are trying to build good associations. In the future, much may depend upon his being confident in water, so handle the matter with sympathy but determination.

It is possible that if your dog flatly refuses to go out of his depth, you will either have to give up or you will have to go into the deep water with him! If this is the case, take your swimming costume with you and some

Morse and the Biscuit

The following incident involved a biscuit and retrieving from water. My friend Christine was picking up with her husband's ten-year-old Labrador, Morse, on a shoot in West Dorset. It was at the end of a very wet, windy, unpleasant day and everyone was tired. A number of spaniels were hunting for a pheasant in a gully and Christine took Morse to have a look a little further down. The river in the gully was flowing very fast. The dogs were not finding any scent at all. Suddenly, Christine thought she could see something caught against some branches in the water. Was it the pheasant or just some leaves? She was aware that the sides of the riverbank were very steep and slippery, and she was concerned that if she sent her husband's pride and joy in, he could get into trouble and she would not be able to help him out. She decided that if she could get him to the spot quickly he would not use up too much energy searching in the current. She always carries a biscuit in her pocket and on the spur of the moment she threw it into the river and as Morse watched, it floated downstream. At just the right moment she sent Morse after it, and it reached the right spot just as Morse did. It was indeed a pheasant and he caught some scent. He picked both bird and biscuit and managed to clamber safely up the bank with both.

running shoes – you may not be able to see what is under the surface. Also have a big towel ready for you when you come out and another one for the dog. If you have other dogs with you, call them up and shut them away. If they are still with you when you go into the water, they will almost certainly want to 'help' you and you may end up with scratches from their claws. The problem dog may try to climb on you too, so wear a thick shirt for protection.

You will not need to go out of your depth for your reluctant dog to have to swim. Draw him in with you and keep him with you, guiding him to swim around you on the lead. You may have to repeat this on several occasions – you can see why it is a summer job now, can't you?

When you come out of the water he will want to have a good shake and will probably enjoy a rub-down with his towel. This is an opportunity for you to teach him the word 'Shake'.

See also the section 'Spitting Out the Retrieve on Leaving Water' in Chapter 12.

LOOKING FOR ANOTHER WAY BACK AFTER CROSSING WATER

Ideally a dog should come back over water the same way he went. However, if your dog is familiar with the area, he may cross the water very happily to retrieve, but then use the dry way round to return to you. You could view this in different ways. If he is carrying a live duck, returning by land may be the best way to ensure that the bird comes safely to hand. On the other hand, if the way round is very long it may be unacceptable for the dog to take the land route as it could involve various hazards and holdups.

Once a dog has discovered an alternative route, he may ever after look for one. To overcome this, you need to train him to respond to you when you indicate that he must return by the most direct way. Send him for retrieves over a stream so that he has no choice but to cross both ways via water. If at any time he appears to be looking for another way back, whistle and call encouragingly. If he is running along the other bank one way, you should say 'No!' and run in the opposite direction. This shows him that the distance between you is increasing and it should encourage him to enter the water quickly so as to reduce it. Any sign that he is about to cooperate should be praised. When he reaches you be really pleased with him. Choose a narrow stream to begin with, and then as he becomes more obedient, graduate to wider ones until he will cross a river. Until he is accomplished and unquestioning about returning the way he went, you should not take him to the other side via a bridge. He will remember it and go looking for it.

When he is going over and back reliably, you can move to different types of water such as ponds and lakes. Start building his courage little by little so that it does not occur to him to look for a dry return route. A good way to do this is to use an island. It should be a small island so he does not waste much time looking for a land route back, and the distance, shore to shore, should be about 10 metres – not too far to panic him but too far to jump. Also, it is probably quite easy for most of us to throw a dummy that far. Throw a dummy on to the island. Send your dog and as he picks it, call and encourage him to come straight back. If he goes looking for an easier option, he will not find it. Be sincere with your praise as he enters the water on the far side, and keep on telling him what a good dog he is all the way.

CHAPTER **10** The Trouble With Quartering

It is important to remember that spaniels, pointers and setters, and the hunt, point, retrieve breeds – HPRs – work out of two separate boxes, so to speak. The first box is all about hunting and flushing, and in the case of the pointing breeds, pointing. The second box is all about the retrieve. The exception is that the British pointers and setters are not required to retrieve, although many of them are willing to do so.

Everything in the first box is to do with questing for unshot game and turning within certain parameters – this is called quartering. A spaniel should stay within approximately 15 to 20 metres of his handler. A pointer, setter or HPR hunts a much wider area in front of his handler, covering perhaps 200 or 300 metres to either side of him. The handler should keep his hands low when casting the dog out, and his whistle signal for turning the dog should be light and short. His whole attitude should be conspiratorial so that the dog has a sense of acting as a team mate with his handler and is not hunting just for himself. You are accomplices in the hunt.

Maintaining the sense of being team mates may be easier with spaniels than with the pointing breeds, as they should work so much more closely to their handler. However, this cooperation needs to be taught from an early age in any breed. In other words, keep your dog within a tight radius until you feel he is working *with you* rather than for himself. This is done by keeping him on a lead at first and encouraging him to run back and forth in front of you, blowing a soft pip (or two pips) on the whistle each time you change direction. Biscuits can be used to encourage the dog to remain nearby. Sprinkled in the grass in the area you are quartering may encourage him to use his nose, but they may also slow his progress or interfere with the fluidity of his action. However, if this works for you and achieves the aim of persuading your dog to remain within a sensible radius, praise can eventually be substituted for food with the consequence that the dog works more freely.

A Springer Spaniel enjoying his work, and all the more for being wet and muddy and out of breath.

A spaniel or pointer should have a fluid action and a pattern that covers the ground efficiently, using the wind and investigating likely areas for the scent of game. When your dog is ready to encounter game scent – that is to say, when he has had a thorough grounding in obedience to the turn and stop whistle signals – it is important to make it likely that he will find scent when questing. Working him across the wind below where he is likely to find scent will give him confidence. Each time he finds scent encourages him and he will work with increased enthusiasm and become more and more fluid.

REFUSING TO FACE COVER

Some dogs avoid cover as a result of being overfaced in early training. If you ask your young dog to go into punishing cover for no good reason, he may naturally decide it is not worth it. He needs to develop a good association with the tough stuff before he is willing to throw himself into it. Why should he face nettles, brambles and thorns for no reward? You need to begin gently and work up to the stings and prickles.

With a youngster, start in soft grass that is only ankle or knee high. Let him gambol about freely, but each time he reaches about 10 metres' distance from you, turn away giving one or two small pips on the whistle. He should turn to come with you, but if he does not, encourage him by bending forwards as if you have found something, and pull up a handful of grass and scatter it around your feet. This should make him curious and persuade him to come and investigate, and you will be able to give a word of praise and perhaps a pat as he comes near. This may make progress erratic at first but as he gradually understands that he should turn within a certain distance of you, he will become more fluid. Bit by bit, introduce him to slightly rougher cover, reeds or bracken perhaps, then something more testing. If you can take him somewhere where there is a little scent but no game, it will encourage him to be braver. Do not take him where he will actually find game until you feel he has a nice pattern and will turn and stop reliably on the whistle.

Some dogs will not face cover because they lack courage. If your dog has been introduced to cover as in the previous paragraph, you may find his courage can be improved by putting small tasty treats in the cover. Giving him easy retrieves in light cover will also make him bolder.

Occasionally you will come across a dog whose scenting ability is poor. Because of this, he sees no point in braving the brambles. I think there is not much that can be done to help a dog with a poor nose. Perhaps if he is allowed to follow another braver dog he will want to enter cover because he learns that that is where his companion has found game.

SPANIELS – HUNTING OUT OF RANGE

Ideally your spaniel should hunt within 15 to 20 metres of you so that anything he flushes is still within range by the time you have raised your gun and fired. It also means that if you are beating with him, he is in an acceptable area in relation to the beating line. To be any further forwards of you means he will be less likely to respond to you if birds flush, and more likely to chase them and thereby spoil the drive.

One of the difficulties with working a dog in the beating line is the other dogs. Not all of them will be as well behaved as yours, and the element of competition may lead him to copy and follow them. If your dog will not remain within the correct radius you should probably put him on lead or he may put you in the head keeper's bad books.

A dog that has been hunting out of range for some time will take longer to cure than one that is just beginning to push his luck. You will need to be more determined than he is. It may not be possible to cure a dog that has always been allowed to go beyond the practical distance, but if he is under eighteen months of age, it is worth a sincere try. You must be ready to devote a lot of time to the venture. There are many stages to the remedy and none of them should be skipped. The following method is likely to take many weeks of repetition before you can see real improvement.

Change the command and the whistle signal you have been using for hunting and start afresh as if from the very beginning. If you have used 'Where is he?' you could change to 'Find him', and for the whistle signal, use one toot instead of two, or vice versa.

Begin each session with a few minutes of muzzle-holding, just because you can. It should help him to concentrate on what you are trying to put over to him. Lessons should last for no more than fifteen minutes, after which you should put him in his quiet place for at least an hour. It is a good idea to set an alarm for yourself, because you may become over-enthusiastic when things are going well, and it is a mistake to go on for too long.

Before you bring your dog out, go to where your session will take place and hide a number of tennis balls at approximately 20 metres distance from each other. Make sure you know where they are as you want to work your dog on to them.

Have him on a lead about 2 metres in length, and walking a zigzag course, go steadily forwards over the area, blowing the turn whistle each time *but just before* you change direction. Be sure to work into the wind, and encourage him not only to keep in front of you but to turn into the wind each time. You should change direction about every 15 metres. Presently he will find a ball and you must praise him and take it from him. The idea you are trying to convey is that he doesn't have to go far from you in order to find something.

Each time you ask him to turn, the dog will probably receive a tug on the lead. The pips on the whistle should soon be associated in his mind with the tug and turning to go in a new direction; to avoid the tug he will begin to turn on the pips. Be sure to praise the dog each time he turns, even if you have physically caused him to turn. Praise will reinforce that it is preferable to respond to the pips on the whistle. Eventually he will begin to turn each time he hears the pips, and after a while he will turn automatically without you having to use the whistle – he will know when he has reached the limit of his range.

When the dog is reliably turning to the whistle on the lead, take him to an enclosure of unmown grass about the size of a tennis court where you have placed a number of tennis balls beforehand. Walk him into the wind in the zigzag pattern on the lead for a while, then blow your stop whistle and when he is sitting, go up to him and unclip the lead. Return to where you were when you stopped him, and after a second or two, give the command to hunt, or your turn signal, and encourage him by walking zigzag again to work him to the pattern you have been practising. Because he is restricted to the small area and readily finds a prize, you should find him amenable and obedient. Keep practising in this enclosure for several days, perhaps twice a day. The wind may change, and if it does, you will be able to work him in different directions. Remember to praise him enthusiastically when he cooperates with you.

The next step is to move to another enclosure of similar size and repeat your sessions there until he is performing well for you. Praise him when you have a good reaction to the turn whistle, but be very quick to scold if he fails to turn. Run towards him in a threatening manner if necessary, *but be sure to stop and change into a nice person the instant you see he is contrite or cooperative.* Remember that dogs can and do react very quickly to a stimulus, which means that they can and should react immediately to commands. If they do not, then you must act. Dogs live in the moment, and they remember what happens in the moment, so *make sure that what you do gives the right impression.* Timing is vital.

Try to keep him moving freely – you want him to be fluid, covering the ground efficiently and thoroughly. Do not be reluctant to put him back on the lead if you feel you are losing control. It is always good to re-establish a physical connection, and you must prevent him from reverting to old habits.

Boredom is seldom a problem when a dog is hunting on fresh ground – this is why sessions can last for longer than six minutes – but it is not always easy to find fresh ground that is also enclosed. To prevent boredom, use small toys as well as tennis balls for him to find.

As you find that he is becoming more reliable to your commands, move into slightly larger enclosures, always remaining in areas where you feel that you are in control. Do not be tempted to rush things. This training must last for the rest of the dog's life or he will be of little use to you.

Eventually you will feel that he can graduate to more interesting terrain. Choose carefully. There should be little or no game scent present, and certainly no game whatsoever. If there is any doubt, leave your far-ranging dog behind and go over the area carefully by yourself so that you flush any birds, rabbits or other animals. As you go, place some small retrieves in the grass. If you have a well-trained dog you can use him to clear the area, but you will have to put out the retrieves afterwards. When you feel you have gone over the ground sufficiently carefully, put that dog away and bring out the trainee on a lead and spend a few minutes talking quietly to him and using the muzzle-hold. When you feel he is paying attention to you, begin zigzag walking with him on the lead for a few minutes. If you feel he is focused on you, remove the lead and commence again with the zigzag pattern.

If you see him go up a gear or two, you can be fairly sure that he has found scent and you should blow the stop whistle and go out to him and praise him sincerely. Wait for a few seconds and then cast him off to quarter again. Turn him frequently and stop him often and really pleased with him when he responds to you. He may become a bit 'sticky' with the frequent stops, but now, more than ever, you are building the bond that will make you into an efficient and effective team. He may not find all the retrieves, but it is important that he finds some so he realises that he should work near you. This session should only last about ten minutes, and even less if he does not settle and focus on you. He should definitely go into his quiet place afterwards for at least an hour.

Stopping him each time that you perceive he has found scent should lead to him stopping himself automatically when he comes upon game and flushes it. It may not be as simple as that, and you may have to return to using the lead to stop him many times before it becomes automatic.

Eventually, through repetition, he should develop a kind of self-discipline and stop when temptation arises.

You are now in a transitional phase and you must not throw away all your previous effort by raising the level of excitement too soon. On an excitement scale of nought to ten, a dog can go from bottom to top in an instant. It is your job to make certain that his progress is gradual and orderly.

A rabbit pen can be extremely useful once you have reached a stage where you believe you can keep your dog within range and can control him in the presence of game scent. Professional trainers often have a rabbit pen and can teach you how to make the best use of it. There may be a charge for this but it will be money well spent. There may also be a fine for any rabbits that are caught by your dog – this should ensure that you take your training seriously!

The best sort of rabbit pen is oblong and about an acre in area. It should have lots of places where the rabbits can take refuge from an over-enthusiastic dog. Sheets of corrugated tin raised 8 to 10 centimetres off the ground with blind sides and end but secured to the ground so a dog cannot force himself underneath are good. Lengths of pipe 8 to 10 centimetres in diameter and 5 metres long also work, but they, too, must be secured to the ground. There should be a pig-wire fence across the pen at a certain point with a wooden bar across the top so that a dog can jump it safely and you can climb over it easily. This fence allows a rabbit that is being chased to escape from the dog. It will also bring the dog up short and probably cause him to bump his nose, which will help to reinforce your stop whistle.

The cover in the pen should be quite sparse so that you can see your dog most of the time. It should not be thick or punishing. It doesn't matter if the rabbits are wild or domestic – a dog will be just as excited by a white rabbit with black spots as he is by a brown one. Sometimes there will be a pheasant or two in the pen that have been pinioned so they are unable to fly properly – these can be very exciting to a young dog and give you a good opportunity to stop him to flush.

For the first few visits to the pen, keep your dog on the lead for a few minutes. If you go in and set him free straightaway, the likelihood is that he will not stop when he should and you will begin the session with having to scold and correct him. This is negative training and costs time. Use the muzzle-hold freely. Ideally, he will not encounter any rabbits or birds on the first couple of occasions. There will be lots of scent. The owner of the pen can advise you where best to go depending on your level of control over the dog. Walk about with him and stop him about every ten seconds. Be vigilant, but kind, deliberate and calm.

Depending on the dog and how focused you think he is, you will eventually decide that it is safe to remove the lead. In the rabbit pen, this should be done near one side of the pen, not in the open, so the dog will feel slightly confined and you will feel more in control. This will give you a confident air, which the dog will sense. Only allow him to go a few metres before you stop him on the whistle; then continue in a start-stop fashion for a few minutes. Praise the dog lavishly for obedience and act swiftly if he does not respond to you. After this short spell, put the lead on and shut him in his quiet place for an hour or more.

Ideally, the next visit to the pen should take place two days later. Begin with the lead on until you feel he is settled and listening to you. Remove the lead and proceed with the start-stop exercise.

Most dogs tend to forget their training when game is added to the mix. It may take several visits to the rabbit pen before he regains his full focus on you. If your dog loses his concentration under temptation, do not take him into the pen but work him around the outside. A gamekeeper may give you his permission to work your dog near his pheasant pens if you ask him. Pheasant pens have 'pop holes' for the pheasants to come and go so you must make sure that your dog is under control when you come near these. This means keeping him on the lead until he is rock steady. It is better to be over-cautious than ruin your relationship with the gamekeeper.

Your dog will find scent outside the pen and become excited, but if you keep him on the lead and praise and scold appropriately, you should presently see that he is starting to obey you. If he does not settle down, you should take him away from the pen, do something you know he will do well, and put him away for that day. Leave it for two days and then try again. It may take many visits, but to succeed, you must persevere.

Hopefully you will reach a point where the keeper will agree to you 'dogging in' his pheasants. This means working your dog around the area where the pheasants have strayed in order to 'herd' them back to the release pen. This will be helpful to the keeper and will provide you with plenty of opportunities to stop your dog on the whistle when he comes close to the birds or flushes them.

I cannot emphasise too strongly how important the timing of your praise and scolding is. Equally, practising regularly and often is vital to making good behaviour and responses reliable. These things combined will make a dog learn his lessons 'off by heart', and he will become a wonderful companion and asset to you.

This step-by-step training requires a big investment of your time, but taking it steadily can pay dividends.

Please note, however, there are some dogs that have had so many opportunities to range too far and to chase game that they can never be trusted to resist temptation. If your dog is one of these, you must face up to it, and he should be found a home where he will not encounter game.

SPANIELS – RUNNING OFF WHEN OUT OF SIGHT OF HANDLER

Some dogs realise that when they get into cover or through a hedge, they can disobey their handler and please themselves. This is a very similar problem to the one in the previous section and should be tackled in much the same way.

Go back to the drawing board and drill your dog in open ground, then on increasingly tougher terrain, until he is word perfect on the whistle. When you decide that he is ready to be tried in a hedge, enlist the help of another trainer or someone who understands your problem. Ask the assistant to walk the other side of the hedge, always trying to keep slightly ahead of the dog – that is, somewhat further forwards than you are. Then if the dog comes out on his side your helper can ambush him with a cross word, which will let the handler know he should blow the turn or recall whistle. The assistant should then make unfriendly moves to persuade the dog to turn back towards the handler. He can tell the handler what the dog's reactions are, and if the dog is responding well, the handler can praise him even though he cannot see him. The dog may think his handler has magical powers and can see him through the hedge! If the dog turns back to his handler, the assistant should praise him too.

Each time the dog comes back into your view you must praise him, and this confirms in his mind that it is preferable to respond to the turn or recall signal. At risk of spoiling some of his fluidity, you should perhaps sometimes reward him with an edible treat. Once he understands the correct behaviour, you can stop the treats and just give verbal praise. If he is a keen retriever, you can

occasionally produce a dummy as he comes into view, blow your stop whistle and when he is stationary, throw the dummy and then let him have a retrieve. In this fashion you can teach him that it is worth his while to maintain contact with you.

THE POINTING BREEDS

The pointing group includes many breeds seen in the United Kingdom – English pointers, English, Gordon and Irish Setters, the HPR breeds from Europe including German Shorthaired and Wirehaired Pointers, the Viszlas and Weimeraners. There are also many other European breeds of HPR, such as the Brittany Spaniel, Khortal, Italian Spinone and Munsterlander, to name but a few. All these breeds are expected to quarter at some distance from their handlers.

These dogs are required to cover a great deal more ground than spaniels when hunting. The pointers, setters and HPRs should range up to 400 metres out from the handler, and 200 to 400 metres from side to side. I have seen them as just a speck in the distance on the heather-covered moor, galloping relentlessly in quest of game scent. When they are going to pass close to you, you can hear a thundering as they approach and the ground literally shudders when they go by.

I have seen them stop so suddenly on point that they are almost bent in half. It is remarkable how this sudden arrest in movement catches the eye of the Guns and dog handlers and the retrievers and spaniels they may have with them. The Guns and pickers-up and their dogs may have been walking along nonchalantly through the heather but they are instantly electrified as the questing dog comes on point, knowing that this could mean a flush, shot and retrieve.

The dog should hold his point, which seems to mesmerise the game into complete stillness, until the Guns are in place and ready to shoot. In the case of grouse, whole coveys may remain in place until the pointing dog is encouraged to move forwards. Sometimes the birds wait until the dog is almost touching one of them before they lose their nerve and burst into flight. As this happens, the pointing dog must drop to a sitting or prone position, and this allows the Guns a clear shot at the birds. For pointers and setters, their job is now done. The HPRs must remain steady if a bird is down until commanded to retrieve.

Although I have not had a great amount of experience of correcting faults in these breeds, I believe it to be extremely important to develop a bond with your dog so that he feels a comradeship with you and has you in his mind when he is questing for game. If you do not have a close and friendly connection with your dog – of any breed – you cannot expect him to be a team mate when it comes to working on game.

Feeding your dog yourself is a good start to a good relationship, but going out together for exercise is even more important. Regular and frequent short training sessions, starting at an early age, also play a great part in forming a bond.

You can teach these questing breeds to turn on the whistle much as you might a spaniel, but you should gradually increase the scope of his range and the distance at which you wish him to turn. It is not easy to run out to impress him in heather, scrub or long grass, so do your early training on smooth ground where you can move easily towards him when he needs a reminder to obey you.

CHAPTER **11** Troubles with the Retrieve

There are so many things that can go wrong in the course of training a dog, but our gundogs, with the exception of our native pointers and setters, have been bred for hundreds of generations from individuals that show a strong retrieving instinct. Therefore there is seldom a need to encourage a young dog to retrieve, rather the opposite! However, problems do still arise – sometimes through the handler scolding a young puppy for taking a new shoe or a favourite cushion, sometimes through insisting on steadiness too early, sometimes from doing too many retrieves while the puppy is teething and his gums are tender – there are lots of causes.

LACK OF INTEREST IN RETRIEVING

A lack of interest in retrieving or in some cases a refusal to retrieve can easily be caused by the trainer as mentioned above. Sometimes, though, it can be innate. In a case where a puppy has no apparent interest in retrieving, and you know that you have not been the cause, I would say that you should be patient and try him just once or twice a week with a toy or tennis ball. You may well find that he will suddenly turn a corner and become very keen. It is similar to some sheepdog pups. For several months a young collie seems afraid of sheep, then suddenly he is 'showing eye'. This means that he almost goes on point when sheep are near or he lies down and stares intently at them. This is a valuable pivotal point in a sheepdog's development. In the gundog pup the interest in retrieving can appear just as suddenly.

In our retrieving breeds, it may be that a dog is very well bred but he has just not inherited the retrieving instinct. However, if you are fond of the dog, you should try to bring him round before you despair.

The retrieving instinct is based on the pack member's drive to bring food home to the lair for the nursing bitch and her pups. As the pups grow, the mother will go out too and hunt and forage for food and bring it back for

her young. The food brought back has sometimes been chewed and swallowed and the puppies will kowtow to the returning dog and lick its chops to stimulate the adult to regurgitate the stomach contents to them. Dogs consider the retrieve, all retrieves, as food.

If your dog refuses to pick up articles and bring them, you are going to have to find a way to make him view his retrieves as food, or at least a source of pleasure to him. Make up your mind from the start that you will keep your temper – overcoming problems in dog training can be very frustrating. I have often had success in building

114

enthusiasm for retrieving by using knuckle bones or leg bones of cows or pigs, but I have found that deer leg bones are the most exciting to a dog.

Using bones in place of dummies can enable your dog to develop his retrieve, even though he refuses to retrieve dummies, balls and so on. Always choose bones he is unlikely to be able to crush, and ones without any vestige of meat or sinew on them. He must not get the idea that he is being fed. Place each bone in a long sock or cover them with strong cloth or canvas. Treat the bones just as you would your dummies. Keep them in a game bag, mark them if necessary so you know them apart, and use a different one for each retrieve in any training session. Keep a few small dummies in the bag with them so that the scent transfers between them, both ways.

You must teach your dog steadiness to the bone from the beginning so that he views it as your property and understands that he is allowed to have it in his mouth as a privilege. In addition to steadiness, his recall must be reliable before you begin asking him to retrieve a bone so that he brings the bone to you when you call or whistle. He must give it up to you readily; you probably taught him to allow you to take food and other things from him at an early age, didn't you?

POOR MARKING ABILITY

Good marking is such a valuable asset. I have had dogs that will watch a wounded partridge glide on for 200 metres or more and when sent, go straight to the fall. They do not take their eyes off the bird for an instant and when they hear their name, they set off like an arrow.

There are dogs that mark well from a very young age and others that do not have this talent. I don't think that poor eyesight is a factor in the latter type. It is just that the dog needs help and practice.

The chief thing when helping a dog to improve his marking is that the handler does not move his body or hands in any way when he sends the dog as this can distract him and make him take his eye off the fall. He just says the dog's name.

It is a huge help if you have an assistant. In your early sessions you should practise in a fairly flat field where the grass is about a handspan high. Give the dummies to your helper and ask him to go about 50 metres from you. You should have agreed on a signal that you will give when you want a dummy to be thrown and another that means you would like the dummy to be picked by hand.

Give the signal for a dummy to be thrown. Your thrower should say 'Mark!' or make a noise such as 'Brrrrrr!' in quite a high tone just before he throws in order to catch the dog's attention. The throw should be high and visible for the dog. A second after the dummy lands, say your dog's name clearly and crisply. You must not move your hands or body. If you have always given a hand signal when sending him, he will probably look at you for permission and probably will not move off the spot. If this is the case, say his name again and lean very slightly forwards or give a tiny flick of your hand. What you are aiming for is that both you and the dog watch the dummy and keep your eyes glued to the fall. If the dog looks around at you for a signal, he will lose his mark. If you look at him, you too will lose your mark. If he goes when you move or flick your hand, try sending him the next time with just his name.

If he will not go, ask your helper to pick the dummy by hand and throw again. You can also move the dog and yourself a little closer to the thrower if you think it will help. This time though, you must use both your hands to hold the dog's head straight so that he keeps his eyes on the dummy. As soon as it lands, say his name and let him go. He may squirm to turn his head towards you but eventually you will succeed in sending him before he has taken his eye off the fall. Sending him quickly may result in you losing a bit of steadiness but you can soon regain this as the dog realises what you want. Hold his head every time the dummy is thrown for four or five throws, each time making him wait a little bit longer before you say his name. Eventually he will realise that he must keep his eyes steadfastly on the fall until he hears his name.

Next, instead of letting his head go entirely, keep the back of the hand nearest to him against his cheek so he is less likely to start looking at you again. If, when you stop putting your hand against his face, he starts to look at you again, you will need to go back a stage until he grasps the idea that he must keep his attention on the fall. You can also stand a pace ahead of the dog to change the picture he is used to seeing when you send him. He may well keep his mark then and go on his name.

If you have to train on your own, a tennis-ball thrower is a very useful tool. Your dog must be absolutely steady before teaching begins. Have about ten balls in a game bag. Send the first tennis ball 20 or 30 metres and a moment after it has stopped bouncing and rolling, send

Hold your dog's head firmly so that he keeps his eye on the thrown retrieve until it has landed. In this way, he cannot turn his head towards you (which dogs tend to do) and lose his mark. Maintain your hold for a second, and then send him on his name but without any signal. After a few repetitions, you can move to the next stage.

This is a stage further on from holding the dog's head. Place the back of your hand alongside the dog's face to keep him looking forwards. Wait for a couple of seconds, and send him on his name without moving your hand. Note that the handler's lanyard length does not allow the whistle to come near the dog's mouth.

your dog on his name alone. If he will not go because he is used to seeing a signal, throw a second ball and send him when the ball makes its first touchdown. It does not matter if you do not collect the first ball before throwing the next because you can throw in a different direction. At this stage, it will not matter if he swaps anyway – you can address this later. If he still will not move, throw another ball, and move your body or hand forward slightly as you say his name. If he tries to look up at you, drop your hand down to the side of his cheek nearest you as the ball leaves the thrower, and say his name on the first bounce.

Once he will keep his eyes glued to the ball and will set off without hesitation on just his name, start to make him wait for longer and longer for the word to go. Once a dog understands what is wanted, it can be amazing how long he will wait, absolutely still, staring at the fall, until he is sent.

LACK OF CONFIDENCE IN GOING OUT ON UNSEEN RETRIEVES

This can be quite a frustrating problem. Your dog goes out with gusto on a seen retrieve but if he has not seen the dummy thrown or placed, he acts as if you are trying to trick him into being unsteady when you give the command and signal to go and find it. He just sits still, steady as a rock.

One of the most effective ways round this hitch is to let him see a dummy thrown, give him a moment to register the fall and then say 'Heel' and turn across him in a tight little circle, insisting he comes with you. Sit him up again, facing the place where the dummy fell. If he sits at an angle to you, say 'Heel' so that he adjusts his position to face exactly as you are. You may need to take a couple of steps forwards so that he moves into the heel position. It is important that he faces in the direction you want him to take. As you come to a halt, place the back of your hand against his muzzle and say 'Sit'– he will almost certainly sit facing forwards. Insist on perfection.

Years ago, an instructor used a phrase that is particularly apt. He said, 'Make sure your dog's spine is in line', meaning the dog's spine should be in line with the route he must travel to reach the retrieve. This is valuable advice. If the dog is sitting at an angle to the direction you

If your dog tends to swing his hindquarters away from you when asked to sit at heel, place the back of your hand against the dog's cheek as you say 'Sit'. Although this dog has a habit of sitting on her flank, she is still at heel and facing the same way as the handler.

wish him to go, he will almost certainly go away at that angle, however clear your hand signal is.

Another useful tip is that, before sending him, you should establish where the retrieve lies and the direction you intend indicating to your dog, then do not look towards the retrieve again, *look at your dog*. If you are looking at your dog you can see where he is looking. If you are looking out towards the retrieve, you may not see him turn his head away at the last moment and if he does, he will go the wrong way, even though your signal was perfectly clear.

When you are happy with his sitting position, and you can see that he is looking the right way, send him very deliberately with a clear hand signal alongside his muzzle and the command 'Hie lost'. He will almost certainly go out confidently. This is the beginning of teaching him the connection with your sending signal, the command, and going out freely on 'blinds'.

1. When you want your dog to go in a certain direction, his spine should be in line with the line you wish him to travel. This dog's spine is in a curve, and she is not likely to go in the direction that her handler wishes.

2. Setting up. This handler has ensured that the dog is facing the way she wishes him to go. She is now looking ahead to ascertain the exact direction she wants to indicate to the dog.

3. The handler has established the destination. She will not look there again but will keep her eyes on the dog to make sure he continues to look in the correct direction.

4. The handler drops her eyes to the dog.

5. The handler casts the dog.

The next step is to let him see the first part of a throw, but as the dummy passes the height of its arc, you cover the dog's eyes. Using the hand nearest him, place your thumb over his near eye and your fingers over the far eye. When you throw, he will see the trajectory but only hear the fall. As soon as the dummy lands, uncover his eyes and let him see daylight – do not wait so long that his pupils dilate – then send him with the clear direction signal and the 'Hie lost' command.

If that is successful, let him see the beginning of the throw, cover his eyes when the dummy is halfway, and cough near his ear just as it lands. In this way, he has an idea of the trajectory and should go the distance when sent, even though he could not hear the fall.

Next, you cover his eyes *before* throwing the dummy. He will sense the movement of your throwing arm and the direction you are throwing. Let him hear the dummy land. If all goes well with that, try coughing next time to cover the sound of the fall. He should go out confidently.

After you have done this several times in several places – and be sure to use a variety of dummies – you should have success when you send him for a dummy he has neither seen nor heard. If he falters, you can sometimes convince him it is worth setting off if you cover his eyes for a few seconds before you send him. If this does not work, you can always go back a stage.

In order to increase the distances, ask someone to help you by throwing at greater and greater distances for you. For throws the dog sees, make sure you turn him in a small circle before you dispatch him. This turns the retrieve into a 'memory', as opposed to a straightforward 'seen' – for 'memory' retrieves you use the very deliberate hand signal, the chop, and 'Hie lost'. You can use the method of covering his eyes and coughing as described above when the dummy is about to be thrown; this also changes the retrieve into a 'memory'.

Here is another way of teaching your dog to go out happily on 'blinds'. You will need half-a-dozen cheap white socks and six dummies. Pull a sock on to each dummy and mark each at one end with a number so that you can tell them apart. You will need a private field where you will not meet anyone else – you do not want any distractions, and you do not want anyone to pick up your dummies when you are out of sight. The grass in the field should be about a handspan high, and it is helpful if there are some tall weeds for you to use as markers. You could use a bamboo stick or plastic fencing stake to lean the dummy against but most dogs quickly learn just to

look for and go to a stake. This is not a good idea as you want the dog to use his nose, to go in the direction given until he finds scent.

On the first occasion, take the dog with you and, using the boundary fence or hedge as a guide, walk along parallel to it, placing the dummies as you go at twenty-pace intervals about 3 metres away from the boundary. Make the dummies as visible as possible by standing them up against tufts of grass or tall weeds or on little humps of ground. Sometimes the ground may be 'poached' – that is, it has dents made by cattle or horses' hooves, and these make it easy for you to stand your dummies upright.

Walk on for about another twenty paces and sit your dog at heel facing the line of dummies. Give him a few seconds to settle – this will allow him to process what you have just done. Be very deliberate and calm in your voice and actions. Making sure that he remains sitting, point at shoulder height as you might for a person, and say 'Mark'. Soon he will learn that if he looks where you indicate, he will see the dummy. Later, the word 'Mark' will be very useful when you wish him to look in a certain direction. It comes to mean that you are indicating something to interest him. Wait until you are sure he has seen the article and is looking steadily towards it. This is called 'locking on'. Place your sending hand close to his muzzle, making sure he continues to stare at the dummy. Give the command 'Hie lost' and the chop signal to go. He should set off confidently.

When he has delivered the first dummy, call him in to heel again and set him up for the next retrieve. Say 'Mark' and do not send him until he is 'locked on'. The second dummy will now be somewhat further away from you than the first one was, and if he does not seem to see it, go closer until you are sure that he has. Because it is white and you have made it stand up so that it is easy to spot, he should quickly 'lock on' to it. When he is staring steadily, send him for it. Continue in this way until all the dummies are picked.

Many dogs cannot count and forget that there is more than one dummy. This is why you must make all the dummies stand out clearly and not send him until you are sure he is 'locked on' to the current dummy. If he does not see the dummy, he will probably not move from beside you, or he will go in the wrong direction.

On subsequent days, start with an easy one, clearly visible and fairly close. With the next one, the distance will be increased and he may not be able to see the dummy at first. Walk him forwards, encouraging him to look ahead

A dog 'locking on'. A white dummy can be seen lying on the bank. The handler places her hand alongside the dog's muzzle and watches him until she sees he is staring at the dummy. Using the word 'mark' at this point will soon become associated in the dog's mind with looking in the exact direction indicated.

When given the command 'Hie lost' with a small chop motion of the hand, the dog sets off with confidence for the retrieve.

with the word 'Mark' until he spots the dummy, then take him back to your starting place, set him up and send him. You may have to repeat this procedure for several or all the retrieves, but be patient and determined. You will succeed.

Each time you practise this exercise, and all the dummies have been retrieved, take your dog home, on lead, and put him in his quiet place for at least an hour. If you have had to walk him out to see most of the dummies, you should repeat this exercise in exactly the same way in your next session. Because he has had time to form a memory of the previous occasion, things should go better on the next. However, this is not always true, so continue using the dummies in a line until he grasps what is required. You could change the venue but otherwise keep to the original format.

You are trying to show the dog that if he *looks* where your hand points and sets off in the direction you indicate, he will find the retrieve. Once you are sure he has thoroughly understood this principle, you can begin to make changes. You can extend the distance between the dummies, always keeping them in the same line. Eventually you can begin to lay them down at an angle so that he does not see them straight away but keeps going because he has faith in you.

On a later occasion, when you are confident that he has grasped the general idea, go to the field *without* your dog and place the dummies. Stand them up as best you can so that the dog will be able to see them easily. They should be in a line at least twenty paces apart, and there should be a hedge or fence on one side to help keep the dog going in a straight line.

Collect your dog and return to the field. You should take him at heel to within a short distance of the closest dummy and point to it saying 'Mark'. When he spots it, say 'Mark' again. Turn away, taking him with you and walk back about thirty paces, still parallel to the boundary. Turn to face the first dummy with your dog, and making sure his spine is in line with the route he must travel, point with your arm outstretched, just as you would for a person, and say 'Mark' again. Bring your hand down until it is alongside your dog's muzzle, and if he is looking keenly towards the dummy, give the command 'Hie lost' together with your hand signal and send your dog. He should go off confidently, but if he falters or goes in the wrong direction, it is because he did not see the white dummy or has forgotten it. Take him at heel back towards the dummy until he sees it, perhaps pick it up by hand and waggle it to interest him, put it down and then walk back with him about half as far as before and try from there.

This process can be tedious but it is time well spent. You are laying the foundations for the rest of your working life together, and it is an utter joy when you can set your dog up, he looks along your hand, you send him and he follows the line unerringly as far as is necessary and brings back the prize. As he retrieves each dummy, if you remain in your starting position, the distance will gradually be building up. He will become more and more confident that you are telling the truth, and will go with more and more pace. It is thrilling to see a dog heading off with verve and drive in the right direction!

In the next phase, you should sit your dog up and let him watch you walk out with four or five white dummies. Go about forty paces and place them in a fan pattern, from left to right, sitting each one upright as you did before. They should be about forty or fifty paces apart so that the direction you send him is clear for each dummy. This will also help prevent him being tempted to swap. The wind should be blowing across from right to left at an angle of about 45 degrees towards you and your dog.

Return to your dog and turn him away. Walk four or five paces with him at heel, and then turn round and set him up facing the last dummy you put out – that is, the right-hand one. He will remember it the best, and any scent from it will soon become apparent to him once he has left you because of the wind direction. Point with your arm at shoulder height and say 'Mark' so he looks towards the dummy. Make sure he sees it and that his 'spine is in line', then lower your hand and place it alongside and close to his muzzle. When you see that he is 'locked on', give the 'Hie lost' command and a little chop signal with your hand. You should not send him unless you are certain that he is 'locked on'. When he has fully grasped the idea, he will 'lock on' even though he has not seen the retrieve, and he will go the way you indicate.

If the dummies are far enough apart he will pick the dummy you have cast him towards. He will be going mainly on sight, but scent will come to him as well. In time, finding scent quickly will give him confidence to go in the direction you indicate even when he has not seen the dummy.

He should go straight to the dummy, but if at an early stage he deviates and seems to lose track, call him back to heel and walk out until you are sure he has seen the dummy, then return to your starting point and try again.

If things go wrong again, take him forwards and when he has spotted the retrieve, sit him up and place your hand alongside his muzzle. Wait a second or two until you see he has 'locked on', then send him from that position, using 'Hie lost' and the chop.

You may have to use this method for each and every one of the retrieves but do not despair, and certainly do not let your dog know that you are frustrated. They are mirrors of us, and he will be unhappy if you let him know that you are unhappy. If you feel that you cannot conceal your disappointment, do one easy retrieve and leave it for the day. Sit him up and collect any dummies still out by hand. Take him home and put him in his quiet place for at least an hour. He will almost certainly perform better the next day.

Aim for success. If you have to make it really easy, so be it – you can build on success but you cannot build on failure.

Another alternative is to sit your dog and walk out about twenty to forty paces, depending on his level of understanding, and place the white dummies at the hours of the clock: that is to say, one at noon, one at three o'clock, one at six o'clock and one at nine. Each dummy should be easy for the dog to see. You and he should be in the centre of the 'clock'. Position him so that he is facing the correct way for the first dummy he is to fetch. Place your hand alongside his muzzle and say 'Mark'. When he has 'locked on', send him with the 'Hie lost' command. As he is about to pick, blow your recall whistle so he has it in his mind to return straightaway and not swap. Ensure a good delivery and then carefully and deliberately set him up for another of the dummies. Presently you can begin to replace dummies or put them at another hour of the clock. You can see that this is a good way for your dog to learn to go off your hand in different directions.

When you feel he has understood about 'locking on' and is becoming confident at going straight off your hand in the right direction, the next stage is to start from ten or twenty paces further back from the first dummy, making sure that it is standing upright as much as possible so he sees it before he leaves you or soon after he leaves you. We are training, not testing. Make it easy.

Eventually you will be able to take off the white socks on the nearer retrieves, although it is a good idea to use pale-coloured dummies so the dog still has a good chance of spotting them quickly. You may think that

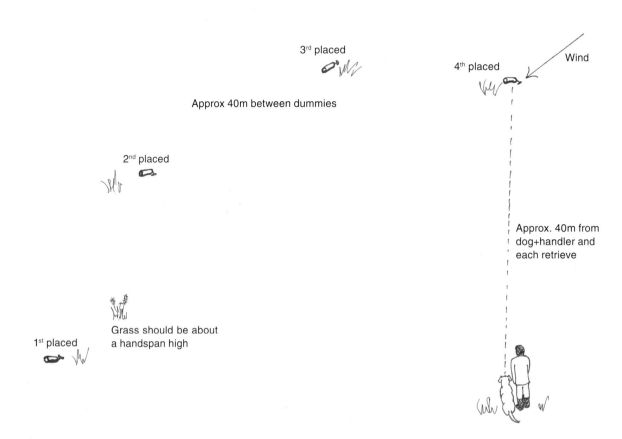

3rd placed

Approx 40m between dummies

4th placed

Wind

2nd placed

Approx. 40m from dog+handler and each retrieve

Grass should be about a handspan high

1st placed

Straight line training. Dummies are placed in an arc or fan approximately 40 metres apart and 40 metres from the handler and dog. The wind should be blowing towards you at about 45 degrees from right to left. The way to tell the direction of the wind is to turn your face until you feel it equally strongly on both cheeks. Allow the dog to watch you place the dummies. The left-hand dummy should be placed first, and each dummy should be set up so that the dog can see it from his starting point. He should be sent for the right-hand retrieve first as it is freshest in his mind and the wind will bring him its scent. Scent from the other dummies will be carried away from the dog, thereby reducing the risk of him taking a wrong line or swapping. Wait until you are sure your dog has spotted the retrieve – that he is 'locked on' – before sending him. The dummy to the left of the right-hand dummy should be collected second, then the next to the left, and so on until they are all picked. When you are sure the dog understands he must go in the direction given, you can begin sending him in varying order. If the dog makes mistakes, you must go back to an earlier stage.

this method teaches the dog to use his eyes instead of his nose, but when his confidence is strong, he will follow your sending signal until he catches scent. Later he may end up slightly upwind of a retrieve and you may need to redirect him, but by this time he should be working with you as a team mate and knows you are there to help.

Remember that you will need to practise this method in several different places before the dog realises that everything is still the same, even though the venue has changed. He must learn to respond in the same way wherever he is.

STOPPING AND LOOKING BACK ON HIS WAY OUT TO A RETRIEVE

If a dog stops and looks back on his way out to a retrieve this usually occurs with unseen retrieves or 'blinds'. You set the dog up, and giving a clear hand signal, say 'Hie lost'. The dog sets off, and after going a few bounds, he stops and turns to you as if to say, 'Further than this?' The temptation is to give him the 'Get on' signal and command, but you should not do this. In most cases, what the dog wants is your attention. If you give the extra command, he may go the required distance, or he may fall into a habit of stopping every few metres and turning to you for that added approval – in other words, attention.

What we hope for when we cast the dog out is that he will go as straight as possible until he finds scent or until we stop him to give him directions.

One way to make your dog give up this faltering is to call him back and start again, but in a way this is giving him even more attention than you would by saying 'Get on'.

A better way is to turn away as if you had not seen him stop to look at you. You need to keep your back to him until he realises you are not going to help him. It is useful if you have someone else there to tell you what your dog's reactions are. Quite often the dog will stand for several seconds and then, as if he remembers what he should be doing, he sets off again.

Sometimes the dog falters and stops through lack of confidence that there is something out there for him to find. If you think this is the case, go out to where he stopped, set him up again, and send him again. If he halts after a short distance, go with him to where he can perceive the retrieve, either by sight or scent, return with him to his previous stopping point, and send him again. Once he has given the dummy to you, replace it in the same spot and take the dog back to your original starting place. He will almost certainly go the whole distance this time.

SPINNING

Spinning is a problem related to the previous one. It usually occurs in dogs with a very lively, impetuous temperament but which have not yet gained confidence in the handler with regard to unseens. It begins when we put too much pressure on too soon. Instead of stopping, the dog goes a short distance from the handler, spins and then continues on his way. It's as if, a moment after leaving the handler, he thinks, 'Hang on, am I right?' and turns, but as he does, he says, 'Yep, I'm going to carry on.'

You need to put the clock back. Make everything simpler. Use memory retrieves and the white dummies.

REFUSING TO PICK GAME OR RUNNERS

It is common for young dogs to refuse to pick game on the first encounter, so you should make sure that you have familiarised your dog with cold game before you face him with freshly shot game.

With a young dog, choose a tidy partridge or hen pheasant to start with – that is, one without any broken skin or bones sticking out of it, and little or no blood on its surface. Show it to the dog and let him sniff it. If he tries to take hold of it, praise him but do not let him have it. Allow him to see you place it in some grass a handspan high about 30 metres from him. Return to him, turn him around in a small circle, set him up and then give the chop signal with 'Hie lost' to send him. When he reaches the bird, let him sniff it, and if he picks it up, call and praise him enthusiastically. If he is reluctant to pick it up, call him and make sure he comes, with or without the bird. If he comes without it, he will almost certainly look back over his shoulder with apparent regret. Sit him up again and send him. If he still refuses to pick the bird, call him up and put him away in his quiet place for an hour.

The next day, put the bird in a sock or stocking so it is more like a dummy, and try him again as on the previous occasion. This usually encourages a dog to pick up the bird. It is particularly helpful where pigeons are concerned as their feathers come out very freely and dogs do not like having the fluff in their mouth. After a few successes you can try him with the bird 'unclothed'.

If the dog again refuses to pick up the bird, go and take it by a wingtip and trail it around just out of his reach. Make a game of it. This should excite him enough to make him try to take hold of it, and if he does, let the bird go and hurry away, calling him enthusiastically. If he still does not want to hold it, put him away and leave it for a week or more. It seems as if a dog will turn things over in his mind and decide that he regrets not carrying the bird. The next time you put a bird out for him, he may well go and pick it up happily.

Do not use the same bird more than twice in any session. If you do, the dog will think you don't value it as you keep throwing it away. After a session, if the bird is not damaged and is relatively tidy you can freeze it and use it again. Once a dog is happy to pick birds, I have found that most dogs don't mind carrying them, either frozen or thawed. This is very helpful because you can keep game in the freezer for use in the warmer months.

Do not, at any time, let the dog know that you are frustrated with him. It will make him think that it is not fun to have anything to do with birds. You could try him with a rabbit – most dogs love rabbits. The praise you give him

When a dog is reluctant to pick up game, it is sometimes helpful to entice him by dragging a bird by a wing or a rabbit by one leg, to create interest. Make a game of it and give enthusiastic praise if the dog becomes keen, especially if he takes hold of the bird or animal.

for picking up the rabbit may encourage him to collect a bird next time you try him.

Even an experienced dog may refuse to pick game of a species that he has not encountered before. Many dogs do not seem to like the scent of woodcock or snipe. In some areas it is uncommon to find hares or geese so it is difficult to give a dog the experience of picking them. If you have the opportunity to try your dog on a species new or uncommon to him, do not hesitate to take advantage of it. If your dog is doubtful about picking the animal or bird, try making a game of it as described above, or ask an experienced dog to pick it in front of him to make him jealous. He may try to grab it from the other dog and it may be damaged, but the sacrifice is worthwhile if it makes him keen in the future.

There is a saying that if a dog will pick a crow, he will pick anything. However, if there is a crow or rook to try him on, make sure it is dead – you do not want your young dog to be pecked.

If a bird or animal has been badly damaged by shot, a dog may be reluctant to pick it. Making a game of it as above may excite a dog to pick up things he finds unsavoury, or you could put an elastic band around the carcass or wrap it in a stocking, which should encourage the dog to retrieve it.

On your first day out on 'the real thing', your dog may not be happy about retrieving a warm bird. Do a bit of stage management – choose a tidy dead hen pheasant or partridge and place it in short grass. If your dog refuses to pick the bird, it is usually just that he is uncertain of what is wanted. As soon as you see that he is unsure, encourage him with praise and call him quite urgently. If he feels that the next thing he should do is come to you he may forget about his indecision, pick it up and return to you. On the other hand, he may abandon it and return to you 'empty handed' – but that is fine: it is important that he comes to your call. If you send him again, he is likely to bring it to you.

However, if he is still unsure, go with him and pick it yourself. Make a great fuss of the bird to show the dog that you value it greatly. Smooth it with your hands to put your scent on it and place it on the ground again. Walk away about twenty paces with your dog and send him again. If he still will not pick it up, ask someone else to send their dog while your dog watches. This should make him jealous. Take the bird and put it out again at a

There is a saying that if a dog will bring a crow, he will bring anything.

little distance, walk about twenty paces away with your dog, and send him again. He may well pick it happily. If not, put him away, in a cage if possible, to 'think things over', and next time you try him he may well complete the retrieve nicely.

If there is no one else there with a dog to send and make your dog envious, and you have tried making a game of it without success, leave the retrieve where it is and put your dog away in his quiet place. Do not let him see you pick up the bird. Let him think it has been left there and might be taken by someone else. This should give him the idea that it is important that he delivers it safely to you in future. Next day, using the same bird if possible, have your dog out for a few minutes' obedience training first, and then bring out the bird and show it to him. The bird will be cold by now and it will have your scent on it. Sit your dog up and take the bird about thirty paces away and place it in some rough grass so he will have to search for it a bit. Return to your dog and lead him away in the opposite direction from the bird for a few paces, then turn him around at heel and sit him up again. Give the signal and command you would give for an unseen – in this case a memory retrieve – and with

luck, he should go and collect the bird for you. If not, put him in his quiet place for at least an hour. Do not tackle the problem again for three to seven days. This should give him time for his ideas to settle into some sort of sense about the matter, relieve him of any anxiety, and make him keen to please you.

When your dog finally brings you a bird, be ultra-enthusiastic with your praise and share the bird without taking it from him for several seconds. When you do take it from him, make a fuss of the bird and then give it back to the dog to hold for a few seconds more. You want him to feel that this is a joint effort with shared enjoyment for you both.

When a young dog first comes across a wounded bird, he may be afraid to pick it up. You should not send him for a bird that is running in full view – it will encourage unsteadiness. Wait until the bird has reached cover, and if possible send a more experienced dog. A young dog's first wounded bird should be one that is alive but which cannot run. Preferably it should be a partridge or hen pheasant; a fully grown cock pheasant can prove to be quite an awkward prospect for a young dog to arrange in his mouth and to carry. Your young dog's

It is good practice when dealing with a dog that is not very keen on carrying game to share it with him before you take delivery. This will build the idea in his mind that you are team mates and are sharing an enjoyable experience. Here, the handler is using a dummy to demonstrate sharing; this starts the team building at an early stage in training.

early retrieves of live game should be easy to achieve – success breeds success. If a youngster has a difficult capture or the wounded bird pecks or scratches him, it could make him hard mouthed or put him off trying another time.

Grouse are a very special species. They are entirely wild, not reared and released as our pheasants and partridge are. They live in moorland heather and they smell strongly of heather. Some dogs catch on to the scent of grouse in a flash; others take a long time to 'get it'. Some never catch on at all. I have had dogs that would happily carry a grouse I have handed them, but when a bird was thrown a few metres into the heather,

they just could not find it even though they had seen it thrown.

DOG 'TOO' SOFT MOUTHED

An inexperienced dog will sometimes be too gentle with his retrieves. You may have noticed that in his early training he failed to take hold of the dummy firmly, perhaps holding it by the toggle or a pinch of fabric as if it were poisoned.

Some trainers say that you should knock the retrieve out of the dog's mouth so that he learns to take a better grip, but

This dog has an unbalanced hold on the dummy, which can lead to it being knocked out of her mouth. The same could occur with a badly balanced bird.

I disagree with this. This treatment may result in the dog becoming handshy or being reluctant to bring retrieves to hand, or may even cause him to refuse to pick up at all.

Hold the dummy at each end with both your hands so that the middle is exposed. Offer it to the dog with encouragement – you could say a word such as 'properly' or 'middle' – and be very enthusiastic when he takes it. The next time he brings it by one end, take it, then place it on the ground and take a pace back, saying your word and pointing to it. After a few repetitions, your dog should understand what is wanted.

It might also be helpful if you keep your dummies relatively clean. One friend puts hers through the washing machine, but I think this is rather hard on the machine. Every so often I give mine a quick scrub with a stiff brush in cold water, followed by a good rinse.

In my experience, most dogs eventually learn to take a proper hold, especially if the retrieves are made more challenging. The retrieves should fall in rough grass or bracken and not be out in the open like a ball on a billiard table. The more difficult they are to find, the more likely the dog will be to grasp them positively.

When you first try him with birds or other game, the dog may revert to taking hold without any conviction. If, for instance, it is a pheasant, you can help by making a bit of a game of it. Have a gentle tug-of-war with him and the bird, encouraging your dog to take it so that the weight is evenly distributed. Eventually he will realise it is easier to manage the bird if he balances it and holds it firmly. This may take several tries and should not be hurried. The dog needs to gain confidence at his own speed.

A pheasant in a well-balanced hold.

PLAYING WITH THE RETRIEVE

The more difficult a retrieve is, the more a dog seems to respect it. If your dog starts to play with a retrieve, tossing it around or tearing at it, do not allow him to retrieve dummies or game that is lying in plain view. Be sure he has to work to find his retrieves. Even marked retrieves should land in tall grass or bracken where the dog has to make an effort to find and pick them. When the dog is returning to you, act as nonchalantly as you can and turn your body so that you present him with a different picture than the one he is used to seeing. For instance, if you usually stand facing him and extend your right hand to receive the article, make sure you are standing sideways on to him, wait until he has arrived, and then use your left hand to take it.

LOSS OF INTEREST ON FINDING DEAD GAME – 'BLINKING'

From time to time you will come across a dog that hunts well, finds a dead bird, but then leaves it and carries on hunting, hoping to find a runner. It is as if he is saying, 'That's dead, anyone can pick that. I'm looking for something more exciting.' This is called 'blinking' and it is not acceptable.

If you catch the dog in the act, scold him, go to him and take him to where the dead bird lies. Immediately change into a nice person and encourage him enthusiastically to pick it up. If he does, make a great fuss of him, take it from him, then give it back to him to carry along while you walk him at heel back to your starting point. Really try to make him think that he has done a brilliant job. When you take it from him, turn it over in your hands and pretend it is a very special prize that you value greatly. After that, you must watch him carefully, which may mean he is only offered retrieves in your sight for a while, and treat each occasion in the same way.

If your dog refuses to pick up the dead bird when you take him to it, you should gently open his mouth and place the bird in it, praise him and then take the bird from him. Make a great show of being pleased to have the bird. A shoot day is not a good time for a training session. You should ask for a couple of birds to take home with you and practise the next day with them.

You should place the birds where the dog has to use his nose to find them, but also where you can see him. If he 'blinks' them, you can make a game of it, as in the section 'Refusing to Pick Game or Runners' earlier in this chapter. It is not respectful to the bird – although it is a dead bird and therefore will not suffer – but it is important that your dog realises it is a good thing to retrieve dead game. We need to account for every bird shot. If he will take hold of the bird, let him know that you are very pleased indeed. Next, place both birds, well spaced from each other, in some light cover. Send him to retrieve and be really enthusiastic if he brings them. Do not use any bird more than twice or your dog will think it is a plaything.

As with any other aspect of training, you should repeat the lesson often enough to be sure that he forgets about 'blinking' dead birds. You must make him know that you are very pleased to receive dead game, so be lavish with your enthusiasm.

REFUSING TO RETURN UNTIL HE HAS FOUND SOMETHING TO BRING

Very often on a shooting day, someone will tell you that 'a bird landed just next to that tree over there'. You send your dog and he goes to the right area but does not find. He begins to hunt because indeed there was a bird there and he can smell something. Then you are told that the bird has already been picked. So you call him but he will not come; he has found scent and he is sure he will be able to find the prize for you.

Some dogs hate to come back 'empty handed'. You can whistle, call and scold all you like but he carries on hunting. Basically, this is refusing to come when called.

If, for whatever reason, your dog refuses to respond to the recall whistle or voice command, you must go out to him as far as is necessary. If you stand rooted to your spot he is unlikely to return to you, but if you go out to him, it will impress him that you are taking the trouble to go to him. A dog knows that he is faster than a human, but the fact that you will make the effort to go after him should make him think that you mean what you say. Scold him in a serious but not loud voice until you have his attention, stand still and then blow the recall again and encourage him to come to you. If he obeys, give him lots of praise and perhaps a titbit, but if he carries on hunting, ignoring you, you will need to go and put the lead on him and reel him in. If he refuses to be caught, do not allow it to turn into a game. Turn and walk away. Apply the advice given earlier regarding the recall.

Whatever way you manage to bring him to you, remember to *make yourself praise him* when you have him near you. He may have made you very cross but you must mask this and give him enthusiastic praise.

Next, leave him sitting on the spot and go to the end of the lead, call him and reel him in again. Do this five or six times, always remembering to be sincere with your praise and free with treats.

When you feel he is complying with you voluntarily, sit him up beside you and apply the muzzle-hold for several seconds. Then send him off to the area where he was hunting earlier but could not find. As soon as he falls into hunting mode, whistle him to come. If he does not turn towards you immediately, say 'No!' in a meaningful tone of voice and start to walk towards him in a threatening way. He should capitulate and head towards you. At this moment you must turn into the nicest possible person and begin telling him how pleased you are with him. For him, hunting is preferable to coming to you with nothing. You have to make it preferable for him to be with you. You do this by being unpleasant when he refuses to come, and being a lovely person when he complies.

The following exercise is a good one to practise and will make the dog more reliable on the recall, especially when you are dealing with a dog that has a strong hunting instinct. You should do this a couple of times a day until the dog becomes reliable. Use many different places, but make sure there is little or no game scent present. Leave your dog sitting and walk away about forty paces, taking a dummy with you. Turn to make sure he is watching you, and as you turn, surreptitiously hide the dummy in your pocket. Make a realistic pretence of throwing an imaginary dummy beyond you – give yourself points out of ten for realism – you have to convince the dog!

Return to him and turn him in a tight circle, then set him up to face where he thinks the retrieve should be. Send him very deliberately with 'Hie lost' and your little chop of the hand alongside his muzzle. He should set off confidently. When he reaches the area where your 'pretend' dummy landed, he should begin to hunt. Let him carry on for about ten seconds and then blow the recall whistle. If he does not turn in response immediately, go out to him in a hurry and scold him. If he looks apologetic at any point, whistle and call again and be really pleased with him if he comes. If he changes his mind again at any point about coming to you, you will need to change accordingly. You need to become a sort of Jekyll and Hyde character, changing from nice to unpleasant and back again, depending on his actions.

Occasionally, when he is hesitant about returning to you, throw a dummy or tennis ball to land somewhere between the two of you and say 'Hie lost' as you do. In a sense he will be running in to collect the article, but he will be coming and will have had a reward for doing so.

NOT RETURNING DIRECTLY WITH THE RETRIEVE – 'RESISTANCE'

Sometimes a dog will pick up the retrieve but instead of returning straightaway to the handler, he heads off in another direction. He may have caught the scent of something else and wants to pursue it. Alternatively, he thinks that while he is out there he may as well keep looking to see if there is a better prize, or at any rate something more interesting than returning the retrieve to you. This is called 'resistance' or self-hunting. Fundamentally, he is refusing to complete the retrieve correctly.

A dog that will come will bring. Go back to basic recall training and do not ask him to retrieve for perhaps two weeks. Make him absolutely reliable to the recall command and whistle signal. You may have to use a small enclosure at first and gradually move to different and larger fenced areas, but do not be lenient with him. He must come straight to you on the first call or whistle, every time. Use treats and lots of praise each time he complies with you. Only when you feel that he is truly willing to respond to you should you begin retrieving practice again.

If 'resistance' has not become a habit but your dog just seems momentarily distracted by something when he has picked the article, a useful tactic is to whistle or call and if he looks towards you, then begin hurrying away. Continue to use your recall whistle as you go. This should gain his attention and he should come quickly to catch up with you. Be sure to praise him enthusiastically.

See also Chapter 7: 'Dog Gone!'.

RUNNING OFF WITH THE RETRIEVE AND EATING IT

When a dog that has been sent to retrieve game picks it up and carries it off, then halts and sets about eating it despite all exhortations from his handler, there is definitely a significant gap in his education. In extreme cases I feel this behaviour is not just a lack of training, but stems from a character fault in the dog: he is innately self-centred and obstinate. It certainly means that he does not respect his handler.

It may be that the dog has not been fully prepared before being taken out into the shooting field. He should believe his handler to be the leader, someone to whom he is obedient and loyal. He should also wish to bring him food as he would bring food back to the den in the wild. To cultivate this attitude, the handler must act like the leader in all his dealings with the dog. He should carry himself confidently and his posture should be as proud and upright as possible. He should not touch or stroke the dog below the dog's eye level.

It is unwise to take a gundog out shooting that is physically or mentally immature. He must reach a certain stage in development and training before he is ready for a shoot day. He needs to have developed a loyalty to his owner. Usually a dog does not develop loyalty and faithfulness until, or just after, he has reached puberty, which is at about ten to twelve months of age. A bitch that has not been in season does not usually acquire the quality of loyalty until after her first heat.

To be fully prepared, your dog needs to have been trained to remain at heel, sit on command wherever he is and remain sitting, and he must come reliably when called from wherever he is. If your dog is not reliable in any of these basic skills, you must not take him shooting. He will act on instinct and enjoy doing things that we consider bad. What he enjoys, he will want to repeat. Repetition creates concrete memories.

Your dog should have been trained to bring cold, even frozen, game both at home and in new places, before he is ever taken into 'battle conditions'. Any retrieve on dummies or cold game that he is asked to perform should be executed without mouthing, and as quickly and neatly as possible, finishing with a good delivery.

If your dog shows a reluctance to bring the retrieve back to you at any point, it may help to put a long line on him so that you can reel him in when he has picked up the article. This will allow you to praise him, which, with many repetitions, should make him understand what you want. When he does what you want, he will find it brings him the pleasure of your praise and pats. He must make the connection in his mind that cooperating with you results in a preferable outcome.

If you have tried sincerely to train your dog to bring his retrieves and he persists in defying you, you must think seriously about whether to continue spending time and

This dog is refusing to bring the retrieve, and in fact is about to eat the bird. This shows that the dog has little respect for her handler and believes the bird to be her own.

Don't Leave Game with Dogs – They Know it's Food!

Game should never be left with a dog in the car, even when you are also in the car. My lovely field trial winning yellow Labrador bitch, Fable, rode home from a shoot one evening lying behind my seat with twelve brace of pheasants I was taking to a friend who prepared oven-ready game for restaurants. On arrival at my friend's house, only 20 miles away, we found eleven and a half brace and one-third of a bird in the back and a lot of feathers. I had perfectly good hearing in those days but I had not heard the smallest crunch. If I had, I could have stopped the car and been very cross with the dog – but as it was, I had to accept that the incident was entirely my own fault. I should not have left her with access to the birds that were, as she knew, food.

---

energy on his training. The dog that ignores his owner's calls and carries game off instead of bringing it, lying down to eat it at a distance, cannot be called cooperative or useful. He will never be a reliable retriever, an asset to his owner. In other words, it is in that dog's nature to put himself first, whereas a well-bred gundog is innately keen to please his handler.

I have had no success in curing this behaviour. It sometimes reduces and becomes a less frequent occurrence, but this sort of dog is self-centred and probably shows it in other ways besides carrying off and eating the retrieve. I would not persevere in trying to make this dog into a reliable shooting companion. I certainly would not breed from him or her.

Some people do talk nonsense, and it can be difficult to sift out what will work and what simply will not. Someone once told me that giving a dog a pheasant or other piece of game to eat at the start of the day would satisfy him so that he would bring his retrieves for the rest of the day undamaged. I cannot see how this would be practical or effective. How, where and when could you arrange it? Would it not confirm in the dog's mind that the game was his and that you approved of him eating it?

PEGGING GAME

'Pegging' means catching unshot game. A very experienced gundog handler and friend of mine once told me, 'There isn't a good dog alive that hasn't pegged a bird; if he hasn't pegged a bird, he's probably no good.' There is some sense in this, as a dog has to have a good nose and be quick and agile to catch an unshot bird, and a good nose and speed are qualities we look for in a gundog. However, we should curb a dog from pegging because, after a few repetitions, he can become expert at it.

I refer you to the sections 'Stock Chasing' and 'Chasing Wild Animals' in Chapter 5.

With a retriever, an interest in unshot gamebirds should be sternly discouraged, much as you would discourage him from an interest in domestic poultry. In the case of a spaniel, he should be on the lead and you should insist that he sits and watches the birds, then moves away with you when you say 'Heel'. With pointers, setters and the HPR breeds, you may be able to use penned game to teach the young dog to come on to point. Again, the dog should be on lead so that you can keep him steady. You need to practise this training on many occasions before your dog will be reliably steady to unshot game off lead.

When a dog has begun to peg game, you should address the matter without delay. Your aim is to teach him that dead or wounded game, which therefore has blood scent on it, is permitted, but catching unshot game is forbidden.

Ask whoever is in charge if you would be allowed to do some training near a gamebird pen, and explain your reasons. Most shooting people will understand the benefit to them in your teaching your dog not to peg live birds, and they should allow you to carry on. Explain how you propose to manage your training sessions, and ask them when it would be convenient for you to go.

Retrievers

Put three cold shot birds in your game bag and take your retriever to an area near the pen but upwind and out of sight of it. This will mean that there is minimal distraction to the dog so that you can have a happy and successful session. There will be game scent on the ground but no blood scent. It is a gentle introduction to your goal. Sit your dog up and let him see you place one of your birds about thirty paces away in some light cover, again upwind and out of sight of the pen. Return to your dog, turn him in a small circle, and then send him to retrieve the bird. The dog should accomplish this without too much difficulty, in spite of the presence of scent on the ground. Ask him to do a similar retrieve in another direction, and a third from a different starting point, always ensuring that the pen is downwind and out of sight of you both, and that the retrieve is not placed where the dog will see or smell the live birds when he collects it.

If you have followed this carefully, you should have had a very satisfactory training outing. Give your dog lots of praise after each retrieve. When he has retrieved the third bird, put him on the lead and put him in his quiet place for at least an hour.

If, for any reason, things have not gone according to plan, try to work out why. Was the dog so taken up with the ground scent that he went off hunting? If so, your next session needs to be in a place where there is no game scent for him to follow. You may need to have this session three or four times before you can go back to trying where there is game scent on the ground.

The next stage is to take the dog on lead and walk him at heel around the outside of the pen. Make him sit each time he perceives or shows interest in a live bird. Alternatively, turn him away, insisting on good heelwork. Giving titbits may accelerate things. You should continue with this until you feel you have the dog's focus on you. At this point you can introduce the retrieve again, starting about fifty paces from the pen. Sit the dog so he is facing away from the pen, and place the dead bird in some light cover. If all goes well and the dog retrieves the bird, you will be between the dog and the pen when he returns. Even though he may be able to perceive the birds, you are in a position to prevent him going straight for them.

Gradually make your starting place closer to the pen. If, on his way out to the retrieve, he diverts towards the pen, scold him meaningfully. However, if he looks towards the pen when he is bringing the retrieve back to you, you should not scold him – you do not want him to think that it is wrong to retrieve! Just call him enthusiastically and move so that you can intercept him.

It is about focus – yours on the dog and his on you – and it is about balance, knowing when to praise, when to scold, and when to keep quiet.

Obviously there may be a problem about the dead birds you are using. You can only use the same bird twice in a session. You may be in the lucky position of having unlimited amounts of game for your training, but most people do not. You can refreeze birds and reuse them on another day, but only a certain number of times. Eventually a carcass will be too untidy or unpleasant to continue using, but hopefully you will have overcome the problem before this happens.

The next step is to take the dog inside the pen. Walk him on the lead at heel the whole way round the perimeter. You should treat any sign of undue interest in the birds as you would if the birds were domestic hens. Say 'Leave' meaningfully and give a tug on the lead. After a few circuits, you may feel able to walk him to heel off the lead. However, this may not occur on the first day. You must be able to read your dog and feel comfortable that he is in full cooperation with you before you walk him free.

Next, start to do short recalls, on the lead if necessary. When you feel confident that the dog is paying attention to you, do very short retrieves, perhaps on a long line at first. *At no time must the dog have the opportunity to chase or catch game. You do not wish to blot your copybook with the owner or gamekeeper.* Eventually, by scolding any undue interest in live birds, and lavish praise when he gives you his attention, you should find that he understands what you want.

When you feel that he is ready, try retrieving on a shoot day. You should only allow him a maximum of three retrieves, and they should be stage managed by you. Ensure the following three things: first, each bird must be dead and not badly damaged. Second, the retrieve should be no more than forty paces from you. Third, the retrieve should be in the open so that you can see exactly what takes place and can call your dog to you as soon as he picks the bird, or if he deviates off line. After that, put him away, preferably in a cage or kennel where he is a good distance from the shooting and where he can settle down and consider how the outing went.

If things went well, you will be able to progress to allowing him retrieves in more tempting situations, but make sure it is a gradual process. What you are trying to convey to the dog is that you are really pleased when he brings you a shot bird, and very pleased indeed if he ignores unshot game.

If a serious problem occurs, such as the dog running off to chase game as soon as you let him off the lead, he is just not ready for retrieving under 'battle conditions' and you must return to an earlier stage. Some dogs will never be ready, and you will need to make an assessment as to whether you should persevere with these.

Spaniels

A spaniel's job is to hunt in cover that is likely to hold game, and when he finds it, to flush it out into the open so that the Gun can have a clear shot. As the game flushes, the spaniel should come to a halt and remain still until his handler bids him to carry on hunting or to retrieve.

Clearly, if the bird or rabbit is reluctant to break cover, it is relatively easy for the dog to peg it. Often a bird is pegged because it is less than 100 per cent well, or the dog happened to corner it in a thick place. My feeling is that the benefit of the doubt should be given to the dog when the evidence is not clear. In addition, the bird will be traumatised by a dog catching and carrying it. It may well be kinder to dispatch it humanely than to release it.

In cases where the cover is light, you can often see when your spaniel has detected a bird. He will go up several gears in his efforts to make it take flight. While working your dog, your whistle should always be in your mouth so that when you perceive that the flush is imminent, you are ready to blow the stop whistle.

If you have worked hard on steadiness and the stop whistle during basic training, it will give you the control you need when the dog is under temptation. If he is not word perfect on the stop whistle, you will have little influence over him when his blood is up. Go back to the basic training of the stop whistle. The rabbit pen is a great asset – *see* the section in Chapter 10, 'Spaniels – Hunting out of Range'.

Do your best to make your dog choose obedience by giving plenty of praise and treats. A biddable dog may well begin to cooperate with you after a short while, but a tough dog that has pegged a number of birds is much more difficult to bring round to your way of thinking. In either case, do not hurry on to the next phase, which is to take him to a release pen.

Having gained permission to take your spaniel to the release pen, be sure to have him on the lead at first and insist that he sits and watches the birds calmly. If he cannot be calm, walk him away at heel until you feel his attention is on you. Do not allow him to build up excitement and become overwrought – he will not learn anything good in that state. Take him away and leave it until another day. Do a small thing that you know he is good at, and then put him in his quiet place for an hour or more.

The next time you take this dog to the pen, only walk him on the outside. Keep him on a check chain and lead and correct any excitement he shows in connection with the birds. Speak kindly to him when he is calm. Stop frequently and make him sit to the whistle. Do this for no more than a quarter of an hour. The use of a Halti (*see* Chapter 8, 'Unsteadiness') may well have a calming influence on him as it simulates the muzzle-hold.

On the next occasion, preferably the following day, start by walking him round the outside of the pen on the lead for about ten minutes, stopping him with the whistle about every twenty paces. Give lots of sincere praise for good and prompt obedience. Change direction frequently. If all is going well, take the lead off and do five more minutes' heelwork. Then take him home and leave him in his quiet place for an hour.

All this seems to be very slow and painstaking, but your attention to detail is more likely to make him into a reliable dog than if you take shortcuts.

If possible, take your dog to the same pen for several consecutive days. Your intention is to have him regard the excursions as 'old hat'. Walk him outside the pen on lead for a few minutes, then off lead, but only if he remains calm and is focused on you. If he is, you can try a recall alongside the pen fence. Only leave him a short distance before calling him, and give him a titbit as he reaches you. So many handlers delay giving the treat until the dog sits, which means the dog is being rewarded for sitting, not for coming.

If at any point the dog becomes excited or loses his focus on you, you must take him away from the pen, do something simple that he does well, and put him away for at least an hour. He must not be allowed to act independently from you – you are supposed to be team mates who work together. It may be hard, frustrating, time-consuming work, but if you are resolute and dedicated you should succeed, and the payoff will be a companion of whom you can be proud.

As time goes by, and your visits to the pen end more satisfactorily, you can begin to broaden your dog's horizons by going to other pens and increasing the distances. If there is a lapse in obedience at any point, go back to an earlier stage.

When you feel confident enough to take him into the shooting field, only have him out for short periods and begin with him on lead. Twenty minutes is plenty. If you are beating and the drive goes on for longer than this, you should put him on the lead for the remainder. Usually the beating line goes too fast for a spaniel to do his job well: he does not have time to investigate each bit of game-holding cover thoroughly. This being so, it is wise to let him do a few minutes' hunting and then put him on the lead for a while. If you alternate like this you will not lose control of him. Rough shooting is much better for a spaniel – you can take your time and allow him to investigate the terrain properly.

The Pointing Breeds and HPRs

The dogs of this group must have speed, nose, agility and above all stamina. Obviously these traits can mean it is highly possible for any of them to catch their quarry. In addition, because they are required to range long distances from their handler, they can encounter ground game while out of sight and indulge in a good chase without reprimand. Another time that it is easy for dogs of these breeds to peg game is when they are asked to 'road in', meaning to move in on the game they have been pointing in order to flush it. If they are too enthusiastic, they may rush in and grasp the quarry.

Once again, the answer to the problem is returning to steadiness training. As in the section above on spaniels, you will need to go back to basic steadiness exercises, gradually introducing temptation at slowly increasing levels. Dogs of these breeds tend naturally to be rather independent and strong-minded – they need that sort of spirit to give them dedication and drive in their quest. Therefore the sooner you address a leaning towards unsteadiness and the chasing of game, the better. You must be more determined than your dog is.

Because a pointing dog is supposed to quarter over considerable distances, a rabbit or pheasant pen will have limited use. A long line or check cord may provide more scope but these lines are not ideal as they usually become tangled in vegetation. They do have some use though, as you can extend the distance at which you can work the dog and yet still have control over him.

Having a good relationship or bond with your dog cannot be overstated.

SWAPPING RETRIEVES

It often happens that as a dog is returning with a bird, another bird falls nearby. He drops the first bird and picks up the new one. It does not seem to matter to him that the bird he was originally carrying was a runner; the new one is too tantalising. The runner, meanwhile, its system full of adrenalin, takes off at high speed and

may never be recovered. This is exasperating and totally unacceptable.

Go back to basics. First, practise with dummies. With your dog beside you, throw a dummy out about thirty paces, and after a few seconds, send him to retrieve it. When he is on the return, throw another dummy over your shoulder to land a few metres behind you. The dog should show interest and may spit out the first dummy but you are in a position to intercept him and scold him for wanting to swap. If you need to, you must pick up the second dummy and direct the dog to pick up the first again and bring it to you. Praise him sincerely for this. Repeat the exercise several times in different places with different dummies until he ignores the decoy dummy.

The next step is to throw out the decoy at an angle and slightly behind you as the dog is returning. This is more tempting to the dog, but you are still in a position to intercept him. Gradually throw the decoy to land closer and closer to the dog's path as he is returning, warning him quietly but sternly not to give it his attention. It is a balancing act now as you do not want the dog to think it is wrong to have the original retrieve in his mouth, so moderate your scolding and be sincere in praising him when he ignores the distraction. Using good timing, and a warning but not threatening voice, you should convey the correct message.

This exercise should be done three times at most in any training session. Make sure that the last time is at the end of your session so that it is the last thing in his mind.

When he is reliable at ignoring the decoy when it is slightly behind you, you can move on to the next phase. After the dog has left you and is on his way out for the retrieve, place the decoy at about 45 degrees off the dog's return route and upwind of him. He will not have seen the decoy being placed but he may smell or see it on his way back. He should be warned by you to continue to bring the correct dummy to you. After doing this a few times, you can let him see you throw the dummy out as he is returning. Gradually you will be able to place the decoy ever closer to the dog's path as he returns, and eventually he will just give it a glance and come on to you. Remember the value of praise and the absolute necessity for good timing.

Graduate to using cold game instead of dummies, and soon the dog should grasp what you want. On a shoot day, you must hope that you are close enough to influence him if temptation occurs. If he succeeds in swapping, and you are able to go out to him, you should take the bird he should not have, scolding him quietly, and put it back where it fell. Then encourage him to bring the original bird. If the second bird is a runner, it is a tricky matter. You must accept it, dispatch it and keep it. When you arrive home, or the next day, go back to the temptation training using cold game.

If you can enlist the help of an assistant, you may be able to impress your dog very strongly and make your lesson more enduring. Your accomplice will be able to throw the first dummy further from you than you can and he can throw the distraction dummy so that it also lands much further from you. When the dog deviates to swap, the assistant remonstrates with the dog and prevents him from swapping. This allows you to be the 'good guy' and also tells the dog he must not succumb to temptation even at a distance from you. In a shooting situation you will need some guile and planning, but you will be able to set up a retrieve in such a way that your accomplice can hide in cover or woodland downwind of your dog's route to the bird. He should be downwind so the dog does not know he is there. When the dog is returning with the retrieve, your assistant can throw out another bird to tempt him. If he deviates, the helper can step out and scold him, and if necessary he can pick up the decoy before the dog can reach it.

Remember to be sincere with your praise when you see what you want to see.

TAKING BIRDS FROM THE PILE

When a drive is over, game is often laid on the ground prior to being counted and placed on the game wagon. Sometimes at the end of the day the bag is laid out in a 'tableau' or display. In some countries this is considered a respectful way to honour the game. With the excitement of the shooting over, dogs are often milling about loose while their owners have a chat or deal with the game. This is a time when a 'helpful' dog will pick up a bird and proudly take it to show to his handler. This is not a terrible crime, just rather a nuisance. You should take the bird from him quietly and replace it with the others and admonish your dog not to pick it up again. Put the lead on the dog and keep him with you.

When you have the chance, take one bird and lead your dog away a good distance from everyone and do a straightforward retrieve. You are trying to make the dog understand that birds that have been placed in a group

by humans are not for him, but a bird that you put out by itself is allowed.

It may be that your dog manages to sneak in unnoticed and take a bird off the pile for his own enjoyment. We should all know where our dog is and what he is up to at any given time, but we all have moments of inattention. If this happens to you, you must hope that you realise before the bird is damaged so that you can recover it and put it back with the others. Make sure your dog knows that you are not pleased. Put him on the lead and point to the gathered birds and scold him quietly. Then take him off with a fresh bird to do a permitted retrieve, as in the previous case.

Guns often leave the birds they have shot in a pile by their peg after each drive. When you are picking up, your dog must learn not to collect these. It may be enough to take him to a few of the piles, pointing to them and saying 'No' sternly before you cast him out to hunt in the opposite direction, but some dogs never give up bringing you birds that have already been picked. If you see your dog heading for a pile, it may deter him if you scold him when you see his intention and he is still several metres from the prohibited birds. If you can catch him often enough when he is just considering picking one of the forbidden birds, he may eventually understand. Your stop whistle may help here, too – if he obeys it, you can redirect him to hunt where he should.

LEG COCKING

It is a common sight on a shoot day to see certain dogs trotting about cocking their leg against car wheels, gateposts, door jambs and so on. They do this to 'mark their territory' and it is not the end of the world, but when a dog does it in the shooting lodge, or wets someone's wellies or trouser leg, it is unacceptable. If you know your dog is prone to this behaviour, you must keep him on a lead from the time you take him out of the vehicle until it is time for him to work. Keep a close eye on him too, as the lead will not prevent him from scent marking.

This behaviour is common in the more dominant dog. Other signs of dominance are raking the ground and kicking up soil and grass, showing his hackles to other dogs, strutting about with his head and tail up when in new surroundings, and vagrancy when bitches in the area are in season. If you see any of these signs in your young dog, frequent application of the muzzle-hold at an early stage may make him feel less assertive. Of course, in the case of wandering, you will have to kennel him or keep him indoors when you cannot supervise him.

If a dog cocks his leg when he should be hunting it shows a lack of commitment to his work and little respect for his handler. In competition, although there is no rule against it, it is considered an objectionable fault, and the dog that does it will no longer be required in a trial.

A handler will soon become familiar with the signs that the dog is about to cock his leg, and should scold him then and there. From the time my dogs begin to lift their leg, I keep a sharp eye on them and they soon learn that I will not tolerate any marking in, on or near the buildings. If you are vigilant, you too will nip the problem in the bud. However, once the habit has been formed, it is very difficult, if not impossible, to eradicate. Castration may bring about an improvement.

CHAPTER **12** Troubles with the Delivery

A dog should regard the retrieve as a privilege, not a right. The retrieve article, be it dummy, feather or fur, is not his, it is yours. Keeping this in your mind will give you the right attitude. His job is to be steady until you ask him to go and retrieve the quarry, to quest until he finds it, then pick it up and deliver it to hand as quickly as possible. The handler must not accept anything less.

A good delivery. The dog has come up close and lifted his head to give up the bird.

It is lovely to see a dog give up his retrieve to the handler gently and without fuss. Some people actually need a good delivery for a health reason. For example, you may have a bad back, or painful knees or hips. Your dog may try to keep the retrieve from you by ducking his head or running circles around you. He may drop the article a metre or two from you and refuse to bring it further. This may cause you considerable discomfort, apart from being very irritating. The earlier you can address this problem, the better. It is a problem that tends to return, so remain vigilant and do not accept second best.

POSSESSIVENESS

Possessiveness is a problem that shows in very young puppies, but can be overcome quite easily at that stage. Whenever you do a retrieve with your pup, always place yourself between him and home – that is, his kennel or bed. Use a toy that you keep apart from his other toys. This makes it an article that is really yours, not his, so he should not become possessive of it. When he is on his way back with the prize, you will be waiting and can take hold of him, not the toy, and praise him while you keep him still. When you do take the toy, keep it for a second and then give it back. This teaches him that you are not spoiling his fun and helps build a good relationship between you. After a few seconds, take the toy again and put it away in its own place where he cannot reach it.

With the older dog you really should go back to an early stage – that is, to the point of teaching the recall. Before you commence this remedial training, you should be sure that you can go through the exercises on three to five consecutive days. Continuity will make the training effective.

Initially, training sessions should take place on the lead. The dog should wear a flat collar. Be friendly and reassuring and do a few minutes' heelwork on the lead. Next, tell the dog to sit while you go to the end of the lead. Take out a small treat and call the dog towards

This dog is being possessive with the retrieve. He has brought it back to the handler but then turns his head away. This can sometimes be overcome if the handler offers a treat in exchange for a nice delivery, but it needs to be taught early on: the dog must not drop the retrieve in order to receive the treat, but must learn that a good delivery is rewarded.

you. When he reaches you, say 'Sit' and, showing him the treat, raise it until your hand is at your eye level. This should cause him to raise his head and look you in the eye. Keep him there in front of you for a few seconds, then give him the treat. Do not let him snatch it (*see* Chapter 6, 'Snatching Food'). Give him plenty of praise and let him relax. After a minute, repeat the exercise. Do the exercise four or five times, and then shut him in his quiet place. This exercise is designed to improve the delivery by creating the habit in the dog of raising his head when he returns to you.

After a few sessions, you should be able to do this exercise off the lead and without a treat in your hand.

Presently you can introduce the retrieve – a small article is best – always raising your hand that used to hold the treat up next to your face as he approaches. Encourage him with your voice. You can use the word 'Dead' as you draw the hand up, and if he complies, you can take the article with your free hand. Some people continue to give the treat in exchange for the article, but this often results in the dog dropping the retrieve in order to have the treat. Usually you can achieve success if you insist on the dog picking up and holding the retrieve until it is placed in your free hand before he receives the treat.

Another way to persuade your dog to give the retrieve to you nicely is to go down to his level. Start by sitting on a low wall or chair and apply the muzzle-hold until you feel he is giving you his attention. He should be on a lead about 2 metres long. Use a small dummy and encourage him to take it from your hand. When he does, allow him to hold it for a few seconds. Then say 'Dead' and remove it gently from his mouth. Praise him quietly and repeat the procedure three or four times. There should be no excitement during this exercise – keep calm and deliberate in your movements. Afterwards, put him away in his quiet place.

If he resists you at any point, speak sternly to him and then repeat your command in a calm, neutral voice. If he grips the dummy tightly, insert a finger behind it and press on his tongue, or you can press on the roof of his mouth just behind his incisors. You do not need to be rough: he should give it up quite freely when he feels your fingers in his mouth. Occasionally a dog will hold on tight in spite of this, but if you press his upper lip quite hard against his teeth, he should let go.

As soon as you have the article in your hand, even if you have had to be physical about it, make sure you praise him and give it straight back to him. After a few seconds, take it again and praise him enthusiastically.

Repeat this exercise for several days, three or four times in a session, each session in a different place. Use a selection of items for him to take in his mouth and give back to you.

Earlier I said that edible rewards are likely to make the dog spit out the retrieve in order to take the treat. However, every now and then you will come across a dog that holds on tight but will give you a good delivery if you exchange the retrieve for a treat. Timing is of the essence if you try this – you must insist that the item is placed safely in your hand *before* you give the titbit. It's a trade.

When your dog is reliable at giving you the retrieve while you are down low, you should begin sitting slightly higher up when you give and take the dummy. Next you can stand to do the practice. This needs to be a gradual progression, from a very basic stage through several intermediary stages to the finished article. It is rather like building a house of cards – one card out of place or missing and the whole house falls down.

After you reach the stage where the dog is giving you the article nicely, go back to sitting on the low seat with the dog sitting beside you on the ground. The lead should be attached to his collar. Restrain him and throw the dummy a short distance, no more than the lead's length, and after a second or two, send him for it. As soon as he dips his head to pick it up, call him and give him a real welcome when he returns to you. If he deviates to avoid you, you can reel him in *so that* you can praise him. Hold his head with both hands and encourage him to look you in the eye. Praise him and then say 'Dead' and gently take the retrieve. Only do this once that day, and put him straight into his quiet place for about an hour.

Some handlers like a dog to sit facing them to deliver the retrieve. This looks nice and it usually makes the dog raise his head to give up the article. However, asking a dog to sit will often make him spit out the retrieve. See what works for you.

You will eventually be able to remove the lead and gradually increase distances and distractions, but always insist on the best possible delivery.

MOUTHING OR BITING THE RETRIEVE

Mouthing or biting the articles you ask your dog to retrieve is sometimes due to temperament – he may be an anxious sort, or the highly charged, excitable type. The muzzle-hold is usually very effective in gaining the focus of a nervous or excitable dog. Be calm and assertive and do not expect more from him than he currently understands. Be very methodical and use 'baby steps' in every aspect of his training. Use the method described in the previous section, 'Possessiveness'.

Some trainers find that holding a tennis ball at chest level with one hand while taking the retrieve with the other seems to take the dog's interest and he forgets about mouthing.

A dog with this habit should not be tried on game until he ceases this behaviour. Most dogs show more respect for the article they are retrieving if they have to work hard to find it, so do not ask them to pick things that are in full view. Place their retrieves in cover, long grass at first, moving on to denser stuff.

PLUCKING OR EATING GAME

Plucking or eating game is one of the worst and most embarrassing things that can happen in the shooting field. A dog may retrieve and deliver dummies beautifully, but when sent out to game, he refuses to bring it: instead he stands over it and starts to tear at it and then eat it. Too quick a transition from dummies to game can cause this. Equally, sending a young dog to retrieve badly shot and damaged game can give him the idea of eating it. Also, as mentioned above, the handler may not have made it clear to the dog that the retrieve does not belong to the dog – it is the property of the handler.

The first time a dog refuses to bring the game and begins to damage it, he must be put away until remedial training can be started. Do not be tempted to try him again on another retrieve: if he repeats the behaviour, you are reinforcing it.

This problem will take some time to remedy, depending on the nature of the dog. A soft and impressionable dog may learn in a few sessions what you want and what you will praise him for; the tough, devil-may-care individual may not respond to retraining at all.

The best results will be achieved if you can set aside some time every day for a week or more for your training sessions. The dog should wear a flat collar with a soft lead about 2 metres long. You will need a selection of dummies. You will also need at least three tidy carcasses – for example, a medium-sized rabbit, a hen pheasant and a partridge. If you have to use three of the same, make sure you can tell them apart – you must not keep using the same piece of game over and over again or the dog will think you do not value it – after all, you keep throwing it away every time he brings it! The reason the game should be tidy, medium-sized or small is to make the pick-up easy. In addition, it should not be bloody, as that would encourage the dog to eat it.

Start with dummies that the dog already knows. Do two or three close retrieves, using a different dummy each time, calling the dog the instant he lowers his head to pick it. If he hesitates at any point to return to you, reel him in with the lead while giving your recall command or whistle signal. Be sure to praise him for anything he does that is correct.

Keeping him on the lead, take a short break; this is to let the successful part of the lesson sink in. *See* 'The Physiology of Learning' in Chapter 2.

The next stage is to move on to game. Suppose you start with one of the birds. Show it to the dog but do not let him have it in his mouth. It is yours. Go to the end of his lead and place the bird on the ground, breast side down. Placing the bird on its breast will facilitate the pick-up. Return to the dog and after a pause, send him to fetch. As he reaches the bird, he should be given a split second to take hold of it, but then you should say 'Come' and immediately begin to reel him in – he must not be allowed any time to put his paw on the bird or begin to pull out feathers. If he does not have the bird in his mouth, that is too bad, but he *must* come to you. That is the vital point – he must come.

Praise him for returning to you, sit him down at your side, and after a few seconds, send him again and act in just the same way as before. He should soon realise that he must grasp the bird without delay or you will reel him in without it. If he has picked up the bird, keep calling him as you reel him in and when he is close to you hold his collar with one hand and take the bird with the other. If he will not release it, you will need to use the method described in 'Possessiveness' earlier in this chapter, of pressing on his tongue, the roof of his mouth or his lips.

Repeat the procedure using the other two pieces of game, and then call it a day. Do not do any more retrieves until the following day.

In the next day's session, do a couple of dummy retrieves to begin with, and then repeat the retrieves with game as on the previous day. On the third day, you should place the game so that it is slightly hidden in long grass, and extend the distance the dog must go for it. This will mean that when you send him, you will have to use a longer line or run with him until he reaches the retrieve. Remember to call him as he lowers his head to pick, and then reel him in without delay.

Your praise is so important. You need to make him understand what pleases you so that he will repeat it, and eventually, it is hoped, become reliable at bringing you game. It will be a long process but if you are fond of him, it will be worth it.

DROPPING THE RETRIEVE JUST SHORT OF THE HANDLER

The chief thing to remember with this annoying habit is not to show the dog the palm of your hand. Always reach out with your palm facing downwards when the dog brings the retrieve. For some reason dogs find this more inviting than seeing the open hand.

Make it a rule that you only accept the retrieve from your dog's mouth. If he drops it, *do not let him see you pick it up* – that is his job. If he sees you pick it up, he will believe that this is what is supposed to happen. If he point blank refuses to pick it up for you, cover his eyes so that he cannot see you pick it up, or you can leave the article there while you put the dog away and go back for it when he is out of sight.

SPITTING OUT THE RETRIEVE ON LEAVING WATER

Most dogs like to have a good shake as soon as they get out of water. They usually drop anything they are carrying, and if it happens to be a live duck, you may never recover it.

When you begin water training, make sure you go right to the water's edge and meet the dog just where he will come out. Bend or kneel down and take the retrieve from him while he is still in the water. Alternatively you can stand in the water if it is shallow enough, so he gives you the article before he reaches the bank. In this way, you can praise him. Do this every time for at least a dozen times, and he will understand that you want the retrieve directly from his mouth and for that he will be praised.

After that he is allowed to shake, and you can, in fact, teach him to shake on command. Gradually you will be able to kneel a yard back from the edge, then two and so on, until he will bring the article any distance and do his shaking afterwards.

The partridge is safely to hand, and the dog is shaking the water out of his coat.

CHAPTER 13 The Trouble with Picking Up

The trouble with picking up is that it tends to get into your blood. You start off with one dog, train it up as best you can, someone invites you to come picking up, and all of a sudden you have six dogs, a 4×4 vehicle, innumerable coats, hats, waterproof trousers, all-terrain all-weather boots, priests of varying weights and sizes, and a selection of walking sticks. This list is not exhaustive!

I have never wanted to shoot, but I love the dog work, and of course, picking up is an integral part of the

Picking up is a solitary job.

shooting day. The job of a picker-up is vital in order to ensure that all the shot game is collected, both from a commercial and a moral point of view. Any game that is wounded must be gathered and humanely dispatched without delay.

Picking up is a solitary job so you must like your own company. There are so many things to enjoy about picking up. Apart from the dog work, many shoots are situated in the most glorious countryside and you are allowed to be in places where normally you would not be permitted. Standing quietly, waiting for action, you may see all sorts of birds and animals you might not otherwise. I have had hares and deer come to within a couple of metres of me before they realised I was there. Woodcock flit by, and songbirds pay little heed to my presence.

The work is one aspect, but the social side of things is a big part of the day. Although you may spend most of the day on your own, it is good to meet up with friends and other like-minded folk first thing and when we stop for breaks. I had an elderly client for whom I had trained four dogs over the years. He brought me the fifth and said, 'I have given up shooting but I still want to be a part of it all; the social side is really important to me. I shall take this little dog and pick up.'

I said, 'But that's very sad – you are such a good shot.'

He replied, 'Well, you see, it's like this. Old men plant trees and young men cut them down.' That was a valid point, but the remark about the social side was very significant.

The excitement of competing in field trials is hard to equal, especially with a dog that is good enough to win, but picking up makes enduring the British winter worthwhile. A good friend of mine who is not so keen on competing but loves her picking up says, 'A field trial spoils a good day's picking up.'

I know what she means. In a trial, even if you do well, you may have only six or seven retrieves all day. At a shoot you may have twenty or more retrieves, some as

Eagerly awaiting the start of the fun.

A good mix of dogs for picking up. Having a number of dogs makes it possible to spell them, taking out two or three alternately for a drive or two, giving the others a chance to rest and recuperate. I have always worked my dogs in this way. It means that a dog does not become exhausted, but it may also mean that he does not become as fit as a dog that works the whole day.

A runner safely captured.

This dog is 'wing blinded'; the bird's wing is obscuring the dog's view and his handler will have to call to him so he can find his way. If there is an obstacle between handler and dog, the handler should move so the dog does not bump into it and hurt or frighten himself.

Many dogs put their hackles up when bringing a retrieve. This may be to put off another dog that wishes to steal the prize.

challenging and memorable as any in a trial. The sad thing is that you are usually behind the scenes so it is rare that anyone knows how well your dog has performed – that is another trouble with picking up!

WORKING MORE THAN ONE DOG AT A TIME

A picker-up needs more than one dog in order to be really effective. Often when you have sent your dog for a runner, another bird falls that needs to be collected without delay. If you do not have another dog, the second bird may well not be retrieved at all. If you have two dogs, you will probably succeed in collecting the second bird. If a third bird falls, your first dog, with any luck, will have returned with the first bird and you will be able to cast him out for the next bird. I tend to have at least two dogs out at a time. Three dogs – usually two retrievers and a spaniel – make a very good team.

Your dogs should have names that are distinct from one another, and each dog needs to know his own name. Spend the summer months teaching your dogs to remain in the kennel or vehicle until they hear their name and are given a signal to come out. It is so impressive and helpful at the shoot if the chosen dogs get in

or out of the vehicle on command and the rest remain quietly behind.

Being quiet when they must stay behind is a very important part of a dog's training. A dog that barks or howls while a drive is in progress will not endear you to the Guns or gamekeeper! *See* the section on 'Unnecessary Barking or Howling' in Chapter 6.

When working your dogs you must make it clear to the dog that you are about to send that you are speaking to him. Your other dog or dogs must learn to be patient and wait for their turn. If one is very jealous and tries to push himself forwards, there is no disgrace in putting him on a lead to restrain him until he understands he does not go until you say.

It is not physically possible for more than one dog of a group to be correctly at heel. When you have two or more dogs walking with you, it would not be right to say 'Heel' because the 'extras' could not actually assume the correct position. Choose another word or phrase – I say 'Come in' – which means 'Stick around and don't wander off'.

FOLLOWING OTHER DOGS

After a drive there is usually a certain amount of 'hoovering' to do – that is, allowing dogs to free-hunt over the areas where shot birds are likely to lie. This is when your dogs will be working at the same time, and it is probable that a younger one will follow an older dog. This is a very natural thing for him to do, and it is quite difficult to stop. Cast out the youngster to hunt first; wait until you see he is engrossed in his quest before sending out your older dog in a different direction. With luck the older dog will hunt away and soon be out of sight of the youngster. Keep your eye on the young dog to ensure that he does not spot the more experienced dog and change course. Encourage him enthusiastically, follow him and be in his sight as much as possible. Eventually the young dog will learn that he can find things even though he is hunting on his own.

If you only have a young dog with you and he is intent on following someone else's dog, set off in another direction and try to keep your youngster's attention on his own area.

I have a special voice command for this free-hunting. It is just a soft whirring sound which originated from the words 'Where is he?' It seems to spur them on and also tells them where I am without them having to look up to locate me. My dogs soon learn that this sound means, 'I have no idea where it is but you have a good hunt. I'm just here if you find something.'

TAKING BIRDS/RETRIEVES FROM OTHER DOGS

Some dogs learn to watch or follow other dogs that are hunting, and when they see that a bird is about to be picked, they barge in and steal the bird. Or they will see a dog carrying a retrieve and snatch it from him. This is based on a natural instinct to take food from other dogs. This quickly becomes a habit and it is an exasperating one! It is very hard to correct the miscreant because he is usually a fair distance from you and he is also near or in contact with the good dog. Therefore your scolding may well upset the good dog. The bad dog will probably think your scolding does not apply to him – he may even think that you are scolding the good dog and that he is right in snatching from him!

This tendency to ambush other dogs appears early on. A puppy will try to take a tuft of grass from a littermate or a toy or food from his mother or another dog. When you begin retrieve training and a dog brings his retrieve nearby, your youngster lunges forwards to try and take it. This is basically unsteadiness and you should treat it as such. Put the check chain and lead on him straightaway and correct him meaningfully.

Stealing retrieves originates from a basic instinct to snatch food from other dogs. Most of our training is channelling or eliminating instincts and this one has to be nipped in the bud early. Treat it as unsteadiness.

You should arrange to have another, more experienced dog present early on in your youngster's basic training so you can show the pup that not every retrieve is for him. He has to learn patience and wait his turn. The other dog may be one of yours or a friend's, or you may be at a training class. It is better if the other dog is not yours because he is less likely to be upset if you have to scold your pup when he shows an interest in snatching the retrieve. If the retrieving dog is yours, he will almost certainly think that you are cross with him and not the naughty youngster. Keep your youngster on the lead and make him keep still while the other dog is working. Tie him to a post so that your hands are free. Remain close to him so that you can influence him. Use the muzzle-hold frequently to help calm him and to remind him of your authority. If he does not respond to this and becomes over-excited, take him away and put him in his quiet place.

On the next occasion, make sure your dog has had a good run to let off steam before the training session begins. He is more likely to be calm and attentive if he has released some of his energy. Apply the muzzle-hold often during the training session and be vigilant – you must notice the slightest sign that he envies the other dog or dogs. You need to be 'on his case'! Sometimes a quick slap on the nose will put him off thrusting forwards to steal the other dog's dummy. A short, sharp shock works better than lots of nagging. Then give the positive alternative and tell him to sit.

You may find that your dog quickly understands that mugging other dogs is forbidden, but he may well think that it is only forbidden when he is close to you. Out in the open is another matter altogether and it is difficult to extend the distances gradually, scolding and correcting every time your dog looks like snatching from another dog. If you are happy using a long line, this may work for you. An electric collar is not appropriate in this situation as you could inadvertently shock the good dog if the bad dog has made contact with what he is carrying.

If your dog succeeds in taking a dummy or bird from another dog, what should you do? If you scold him, it may make him think it is wrong to retrieve. It could make him anxious and this may lead to hard mouth. It is probably best just to take the retrieve as amiably as you can – at least you may have a nice delivery.

With luck, the dog that originally picked the retrieve may not be a pushover and he will tell the thief off or even 'go for' him. This may dissuade the naughty dog from trying to steal on a future occasion. I have known dogs that relinquish their retrieve to the thief quite happily – it is as if they are pleased that someone else is going to carry it.

ETIQUETTE

A shoot only exists because of the Guns. They are the most important people there. If a Gun has a dog with

The picking up team returning to the game cart.

him, the pickers-up should defer to him. Go up and ask if he wishes to pick his own birds. Usually the reply is that he would like his dog to pick the dead birds around his peg but would like you to pick the runners. Some Guns are adamant that they do not want a picker-up anywhere near them. If you upset a Gun, your welcome on that shoot may be no more. Should your dog run in on a Gun's bird, do not delay in going to apologise – most people will come halfway to an apology. Keep your distance after that and keep your dog on the lead.

You may argue that you have been asked to the shoot to do a job, and this is true, but every sphere has its rules and it is vital to the smooth running of a shoot day that etiquette is observed. Without the Guns there would be no shoot, so they come first.

Some shoots prefer the picking up to be done after the drive has ended. Others are keen to have runners collected during a drive, but only if dogs do not go in front of the Guns and distract them. You should ascertain what your head keeper likes before the season begins. Do not ask him on the morning of the shoot, when he needs to concentrate on running the day.

In case there is some sort of problem or an emergency, make sure to have your mobile phone with you when you go picking up – but be sure to turn off the ringer when you are anywhere near the Guns. Some shoots provide radios and they may be on the same frequency as the head keeper's and beaters' radios. If they are, you must not speak during a drive. If radios are not provided, it is not very expensive for the picking-up team to buy their own set. Again, when you are near the Guns, the volume should be turned down or off, and do not use them during a drive.

NEVER HAVE A TIRED DOG

As mentioned above, if you are serious about picking up, you will need more than one dog, preferably three or more. A four-wheel-drive vehicle is a great asset. It means that you can go to almost all parts of the shoot, and this will enable you to swap dogs over to keep them from becoming overtired. Working each dog in every other drive will preserve their energy. Possibly you may need to put an injured dog into a safe place quickly, or even take him to the vet – another advantage of having the 'dog-mobile'.

The cab of this vehicle has had dividers installed to prevent excessive movement of precious cargo. The compartments enable the handler to keep dogs separate in cases where, for instance, dogs are unfriendly or when a bitch resents the attentions of a forward male. It is easier with this arrangement to call out the dogs you want when others are too eager.

Drinking water helps to maintain stamina so make sure your dog has access to clean water frequently during the working day. Always carry dextrose tablets or honey sandwiches to give to your dogs when you feel they need a boost. Towelling or fleece coats that are put on between drives, at lunchtime and at the end of the day mean a dog does not have to waste energy keeping warm, and I believe will prolong his working life. You must be able to put your dog into a warm, comfortable place during elevenses, or the lunch break; many dogs become chilled, even hypothermic, on a cold wet day if they have to stand about for any length of time.

If your vehicle is the twin-cab type, crates or dividers will ensure the dogs do not have too much room to be thrown about when you are going over rough terrain, or when you are driving at speed and may have to brake suddenly. The floor and other hard surfaces should be cushioned to prevent injury.

As a picker-up you will often be left behind because you have been looking for a hard-to-find bird. By the time you catch up with the other members of the shoot they will have finished their elevenses or lunch, so having your own snacks and a drink in your vehicle will keep you going.

Waiting for the fun to begin.

CHAPTER **14** Condition, Injuries and Age

BUILDING UP AND MAINTAINING CONDITION

A gundog needs to be very fit to stand up to a full day's work in the shooting field. Build up his fitness and stamina gradually over the few months before the start of the season. He should be lean and well muscled so that he is agile and sure-footed. We should make an effort to be physically ready too, of course! As we all know, being fit is not the same as being 'match fit', so be careful your dog does not overdo it in the early days of the season.

He should be fed a good quality ration. Feed according to condition. If he is looking too prosperous, cut back his food and add more water to it so he feels full. A dog needs a little reserve to fall back on if he becomes unwell, but if he is overweight you should acknowledge this, and

make sure he is in good condition for work. Many young gundogs seem to prefer to look like a lurcher for the first two to three years of their life. If your dog is showing a lot of ribs, feed more and perhaps more often. Dogs fed twice a day make better use of their food than those fed only once. Certain complete foods contain high levels of oil, and cooked, boned neck and breast of lamb is a good source of fat. Adding these to your dog's regular food should help him to gain weight.

Dry food must become wet by some means so that a dog can digest it. This is achieved either by the dog drinking water or the person who feeds him wetting the food before giving it to him. If you use a complete food, wetting it with warm water before feeding will make it more easily digestible than feeding it dry. After all, where in Nature would a dog encounter dry food?

These four dogs are fit and well muscled, ready for work. And don't underestimate the grey-muzzled old boy: he may be slower but he has stamina and experience.

These feet are right for work. They are neat and the nails are trim. The hair between the toes of the right-hand dog has been left as I believe it to be natural protection against thorns and injury.

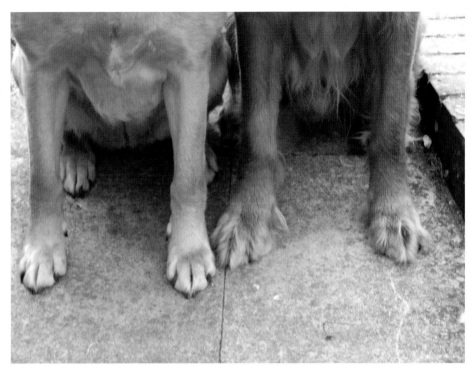

A dry bone, yes, but that is not what we mean when we speak of food.

Before the season begins, ask your veterinarian for the right sort of parasite treatments so that your workmate is not carrying a worm, flea or tick burden. Dogs work better if they are on peak form.

Spaniels and some other long-haired dogs should have the long hair of their ears made short and tidy so they do not pick up burrs and brambles easily. Trimming their leg and tail feathering helps against this too. I do not trim between the toes as I believe this makes it easier for grass seeds to make their way in; this can be a serious problem as the seeds can work their way into the dog's flesh. Other owners believe the opposite and trim their long-haired dogs' feet very neat and tidy. Make sure your dog's nails are kept neat and short – too long and they can catch in wood, stones or undergrowth, and break or even be torn off. This is extremely painful for the dog, and can take weeks to heal.

When he is working, an energy snack at 'half time' will give him a boost. Commercially made energy bars are available, but sardine sandwiches or a banana are cheap alternatives. Some shoots have water troughs in every field; others are 'dry shoots'. Make sure you provide drinking water often during the day. You must notice when your dog is tired or has been overfaced, and put him away somewhere snug for one or two drives. If he is cold or wet, put a coat on him. A coat means your dog will not use energy trying to keep warm, and he will recover more quickly from the exertions of the day. Unless the weather is warm, he should wear a coat during refreshment breaks and on the journey home. Check him carefully for thorns and injuries at the end of the day.

Some owners believe a dog should rest for at least an hour after work before feeding him, but I feed mine when I reach home. A dog in the wild would not wait for an hour to devour the prey he has worked hard to catch; he would consume as much of it as he could and as soon as possible before someone else came along to steal it!

At the end of the season, working dogs are very fit. The season comes to an abrupt stop. A fit dog will be almost jumping out of his skin and won't know what to do with his energy. You should 'let him down' gradually by taking him out for long walks, or frequent short ones, or he may become destructive or noisy due to boredom.

Training sessions will be a good way of occupying his mind and body.

Your dog could be kept at the peak of fitness all year round but I feel that some 'down time' is of benefit to both dog and handler.

DEALING WITH INJURIES

There are many possibilities for injuries on a shoot day; in fact it is remarkable that accidents do not occur more often than they do. Keeping a book on first aid and a first-aid kit in your vehicle is well worthwhile. On the lid of the kit should be your vet's name and telephone number. If you are away from your district, ask for the name and number of the vet local to the shoot, write it down or put it in your phone.

In the kit, as well as the usual bandages, cotton wool, scissors, tweezers, a syringe, antiseptic fluid and cream,

---

Be Prepared: Fences

I once had a dog catch her leg in a fence. When jumping, she had put her hind leg through the fence on the take-off side and her body finished up hanging on the other side. She was panicking and I knew I should cover her head with my coat so I would not be bitten when trying to help her, but I didn't and she bit me. However, I was able to pitch her back over the fence, which freed her. I told her to sit, gave her two arnica pills and took two myself. She did not limp afterwards and the pain of the bite she had given me quickly went away.

On another occasion my Flatcoat jumped awkwardly and became hung up on wire by two toes of a back foot. He shrieked once, then hung there. Such a kind dog – he kept still when I told him to and did not bite me, but he was too heavy for me to lift so I phoned a friend to come and help and asked him to bring wire cutters. He cut the wire while I took the weight as best I could. Understandably, I recommend that you keep your mobile phone with you and carry a multi-tool.

---

there should be a comb for removing bees or wasps from your dog's coat, and an anti-histamine recommended by your veterinary surgeon. Another useful item to have with you is a multi-tool or wire cutters. My kit includes a waterproof, tough boot that has come in useful when a dog has cut a pad. I always carry arnica pills as I have found them effective both for the dog and for me against the pain of a knock or bruising.

Water Tail

There is a condition known variously as water tail, horse tail, wooden tail, drop tail and even Labrador tail, which occurs quite commonly in gundogs, especially Labradors and Golden Retrievers. This causes obvious discomfort and malaise. The dog holds his tail like a horse, and moving it is very painful to him. The condition is usually caused by the dog having been swimming, or can be caused just from being wet. Drying your dog thoroughly after stormy weather or water work may help. However, I have known this condition affect dogs even after they have been bathed and carefully dried. Occasionally it can be the result of backing into something hard or having been bumped by another dog. Even with painkillers and anti-inflammatory drugs, this condition can last for ten days or more. Training the dog during this time is futile and expecting him to work is unkind. Keep him warm and dry and be patient.

Cuts and Tears

Cuts and tears can look very alarming because of the blood. The thing about blood is that it is so red, and a little goes a long way. However, things are usually not as bad as they look. Nevertheless, if the bleeding is profuse you must suspect that a main vessel is damaged. Pressure should be applied to stem the flow. The dog must reach a veterinarian as soon as possible.

In the case of a cut or tear, the main consideration is to make sure that the injury is clean and that there is no speck of debris in it. Wash it out with clean water and antiseptic if possible. Apply antiseptic cream if you have it. With injured ears, pads and tails, it is wise to bandage them as soon as possible so that the blood is not spattered far and wide. Dogs wag their tails and shake their heads and their feet soon cover a large area. If the wound is a puncture, be sure to flush it thoroughly with a dilute antiseptic solution as soon as possible. Use a warm solution and syringe it gently into and all around the inside of the wound.

Sometimes a wound may require stitches and a course of antibiotics. If you are undecided, your veterinary surgeon is the best judge of what should be done. A trip to the surgery at the end of a shooting day is about the last thing you want, but we rely on our dogs for their talents and our enjoyment – we owe it to them.

Dog Run Over

Thankfully, a dog being run over by a vehicle is not common on a shoot day, but occasionally it does happen. It is sometimes difficult to assess the seriousness of the injuries so it is best to take the dog to your veterinary surgeon as soon as possible, even if the dog gets up and appears to be all right. Internal bleeding must be suspected if the dog collapses without obvious external signs. The eye rims and gums will be an ominous grey or white. Veterinary attention must be sought immediately.

Damage to the Eyes

Particles of dirt, insects and bits of debris can be syringed out of the eye with a saline solution. Small sachets of this can be obtained from your chemist to be used for both the dog and you. A bramble or thorn scratch across the surface of a dog's eye can look ugly, but this sort of injury will heal in a week or two. A thorn or spike can go into the eyeball itself, or in alongside it. This definitely needs to be seen by your veterinarian as quickly as you can manage it.

Snake Bite

If a dog is bitten by a snake, you must take him to the veterinary surgeon as soon as you can.

MANAGING BITCHES

It is not considerate to bring bitches in season to a shoot unless you are certain that none of the other dogs are male. Even then, you must keep careful watch in case a local collie suddenly appears!

Some people think you should wrap your pregnant bitch in cotton wool, but it should be remembered that labour is hard work and the bitch needs to be fit when her puppies arrive. Pregnant gundog bitches can usually work up until the fourth or fifth week of gestation, though it is probably best to restrict them to level ground and light cover. It is probably safe to allow your bitch to negotiate little jumps and banks, but expecting her to go over or through five-bar gates is definitely not a good

idea. Swimming and long periods in the water can be exhausting – exercise should be kept at a moderate level. Your bitch and her litter are valuable so you should not take risks.

WORKING A YOUNG DOG

A shooting day should be fun for all involved. Your dog should be an asset, not a nuisance.

If he has not been carefully trained to a certain standard the young dog should not be taken out in the shooting field. Without sufficient training or experience he may become frightened, and it could take a long time for him to gain enough confidence to enjoy his outings or be a useful companion. On the other hand, he may enjoy it all so much that he loses his head completely. Adrenalin will course through his system and the excitement of his first outing will never be forgotten. No matter how much training you put in after that, he will remember the intoxication of that first day and he may never become reliable in that environment. He will not be the dog to make you proud. You and he may become known far and wide for his unruly behaviour. Do the groundwork and be objective and patient.

Your young dog should be steady off lead at heel and in the sit, and should come without hesitation when called or whistled. He should have been taught not to chase. He should have been out training in company with other dogs and people, and should be used to the sound of gunfire. He should be accustomed to retrieving cold game. He needs to have learnt patience – it is not always his turn.

The first few times you take your young dog out, it is best that you do not carry a gun. You need to give him your undivided attention. In spite of all the work you have put in, he may find his first shoot too overwhelming, and may seem to have forgotten all his lessons. If this is the case, try taking him away from the shooting and make sure that you choose a spot to stand where birds will not be falling close to you. He will be able to hear and see the action, but the distance should make the situation less stimulating. If he will not become calm, take him home, if possible, or put him where he cannot hear or see what is going on. You will need to go back several stages in his training and delay his exposure to shooting for some time, perhaps until the following season.

Another aspect of working a young dog is that of not putting too much stress on his joints. Medium-sized or

Calypso. At ten weeks she is too young to go out in the shooting field, but with her breeding she should train easily and be out in around a year.

large breeds of dog tend not to be physically mature until twelve to eighteen months of age. We hope a dog's working life may extend to ten or twelve years, and it would be a shame to cause the early onset of arthritis by giving him too much work at an early age.

THE ELDERLY DOG

Many gundogs are able to work well until they are ten years or older, providing they have been kept fit, fed well but not too much, and do not have health problems such as arthritis or a bad heart. The older dog will often find game that younger ones have missed – they are experienced, thorough, and usually steadier, and they should not be underestimated.

A dog that has become hard of hearing may seem unable to locate where your calling or whistling is coming from – he appears to hear you, but sets off in the wrong direction. Many dogs have a habit of checking on you regularly and often; these can be given a signal to encourage them to come your way. A truly deaf dog can be quite a liability on a shooting day as it is easy for him to lose you. It is a very hard decision to make, but there comes a time when he is best left at home. Perhaps he can be driven about in the vehicle if he will wait there quietly during drives. He can be let out at break time and join in the social side.

Surprisingly, blind dogs can and do work well. A friend of mine had a cocker spaniel that lost her sight after an accident. She was equipped with a pair of Doggles – goggles for dogs – which protected her eyes from sticks and twigs. Somehow she seemed able to sense and avoid larger obstacles such as trees and walls.

You will know your dog better than anyone else, and as always, will be able to 'read' him and see when he has had enough. Give him special attention at the end of the day. Check for thorns and injuries. Drinking water is very important. Make sure he is warm and dry for the journey home, and that he has a warm meal waiting for him there.

TAILPIECE

You may have found, having read this book, that I have not covered your particular problem. However, I firmly believe that most training problems can be cured or lessened by certain basic principles. Often you must go back a stage or several stages. You will need to plan your sessions and include a back-up plan in case things do not go well. You may need to devote more time to training than you ever expected. You will almost certainly have to change your approach. If you are dedicated and determined, you should achieve success or, at any rate, improve matters.

We are always learning, and it is a wonder this manuscript ever reached the publisher as I kept on learning new ways to tackle the many hiccups encountered in training. You will discover new ways too, so keep an open mind and a listening ear!

If you encounter a serious problem that you cannot overcome, one that makes you decide that the dog is not going to 'make the grade', a good home can usually be found for him. In time, a dog that suits you better will be found.

Having said that, if you have become very fond of a dog and you feel that his fault is one you can live with, you can, of course, make a compromise. It is all in degree. All dogs have their talents and merits. For example, I have a very well-bred and good-looking Labrador bitch that I do not take to shoots because she is noisy – but she is the most marvellous house dog: she never steals, does not push doors open, get on the furniture nor chew my belongings. Her best point is that she gives a few barks if anyone is about, for which I am grateful, so she will stay. I have a Flatcoat who never agrees with me about directions or steadiness, but which is a friend who makes me laugh and is the most amazing gamefinder: he had a ten-dog eyewipe one day! So he's a 'keeper'.

Life is full of compromises, but in the long run we should enjoy our dogs, and they should be happy to be in our company.

Handler and dogs in tune.

GLOSSARY

backing In the pointing breeds, when one dog comes on point, others quartering with him should 'honour' the first dog's point by mimicking him and stopping as well.

bag The total amount of game shot and collected on the day.

blinking When a dog finds a retrieve but refuses to pick it, sometimes because he is unfamiliar with it, sometimes through obstinacy.

coming on point/pointing When a pointing dog perceives game by scent, he halts with his nose pointing towards the position of the game. He should remain 'frozen' until his handler encourages him forward to flush.

dogging in Using a dog to persuade game birds, usually pheasants, to return to their home wood or pen.

dropping to flush When game flushes, the dog should sit or lie down so as not to spoil the Gun's shot.

flush When a dog puts game to flight – for example, makes a rabbit break from his seat, or causes a bird to take wing.

Gun Person shooting.

hold his ground To persevere in hunting the area where the game or retrieve is believed to be, or to concentrate on an area and not widen his search.

holding his point/staunch on point When a pointing dog has come on point, he remains still until bidden by his handler to move forward to flush the game.

peg (noun) A Gun's number peg.

peg (verb) When a dog catches an unshot bird or other game.

peg dog A dog that stays quietly by his handler's peg during the drive without being tethered.

priest A short, weighted stick used to dispatch game.

road in When the pointing dog is encouraged forward by his handler in order to flush the game he has been holding.

running in Going to retrieve before being sent.

scent marking Urinating by dogs and bitches to mark 'their' territory.

INDEX